UNLIKELY

Ruhanga neiha abantu omu omurituro.

UNLIKELY

A Memoir by Uncle Ben

INAKA
· WRITERS HAVEN ·

First published in Uganda in 2022 by Benoni Mugarura-Mutana

1 3 5 7 9 25 24 23 22

ISBN: 973-9913-9997-0-0

First paperback edition: February 2022

Compilation & Research by Paul B. Mugarura-Mutana
Edited by Gloria Bwandungi Mugarura
Cover art & Layout by Gloria Bwandungi Mugarura
Brought to Print by

INAKA
• WRITERS HAVEN •

an imprint of Tokra Innovation (U) Ltd.
P.O. Box 101565, Kampala, Uganda.
Printed in Uganda

For Akachuramutima

Foreword

My name is Benoni Mugarura-Mutana. I spent most of my adult life working with youth and young adults. My wife, Joyie, and I live in a small town off Hoima Road, outside Uganda's bustling capital city. In retirement we still spend our time, money, and use our property to further our hearts' desire: raise a generation of young leaders passionate about their faith. They are the future leaders of our nation.

The Lord blessed us with three acres of beautiful land overlooking lush neighbouring hills where we built our retirement home, and a leadership training centre. The Joy Centre wouldn't exist without the friendship and generous support of countless people around the World, whose names would fill many hundreds of pages. You are precious to us.

Over many years, God has carefully written the improbable story of our lives, turning every challenge into a unique opportunity to inspire others, no matter their station in life. Joyie and I understand that the purpose of our lives is to help you, wonderful child of God, realize that God's story for you is bigger and more marvellous than even you could ever imagine for yourself.

It has been the privilege of my life to lead and pastor thousands of youth. I have witnessed the hand of God move in miraculous ways to provide for my family, and open unimaginable doors with opportunities for service lurking within. I have preached in small, rural congregations, and stood on huge platforms in large stadiums filled with hundreds of eager listeners. God granted me the opportunity to give quiet counsel to influential people and watch as they succeeded or failed after ignoring my advice.

Loving couples eager to begin their lives together have flourished under my counsel. I stood with them at the altar when they vowed their faithfulness and love to each other, their families watching on in joy. God granted me the ability to be present and a comfort to families in their time of bereavement. Children swathed in baptismal clothes squirmed in my arms, bawling at the shock of water sprinkled on their foreheads while their anxious parents looked on. And the blessing of watching them grow into formidable and successful adults makes my heart joyful.

This journey through the ministry God placed on my heart amazes me every single day. He chose me, despite my humble beginnings, even through my mistake-filled youth. He chose me. He placed me where I am today.

Often in our conversations and musings, Joyie and I are reminded of the transformation of our lives by a Savior who saw it fit to work through us for his Glory. We adopted a principle that continues to guide our lives; a simple directive from God.

This is the word of the Lord to Zerubbabel: 'Not by might nor by power, but by my Spirit,' says the Lord Almighty.

- Zechariah 4:6

This is not the triumphant story of a hero racing towards enemies and vanquishing them in glorious battle, nor is it the rags-to-riches story of a man driven to climb to the top of society. I'm here because many years ago God's Spirit interrupted the self-destructive life of a young adult facing the gaping jaws of death. In these pages, you'll not find the story of a powerful man wielding his influence to affect change by the strength of his will. I am only possible because God's Spirit cleared a path so I might serve him whenever I step through doors He opens. This is the unlikely tale of a man whose path to the present was set in motion by the work of the Spirit of the Lord.

Let's take the twisted journey through it by starting at the beginning, flipping the pages to the years before my birth, to the lives of the greatest influence of my childhood. Let's dip our toes in my Grandfather Mutambuka's history, sit awhile with my father, Blasio Runyasi Mutana, and my mother Nyabuzaana Kenyanje Tofasi Margaret Mutana.

Circa 1967, Bishop Tucker School of Divinity, Kampala.

1

Unlikely Beginnings

Most people know me as Uncle Ben or as Ben, but my birth name is Mugarura. I was born into a polygamous family. My mother was my father's first wife. Six children survived her reluctant womb, and the ravages of unresolved childhood illness. I am the fifth of her gaggle of children. Our father gave each of us a name significant to the events surrounding our birth, or commensurate with his joy at seeing our cherubic faces.

The first fruit of my parents' union was Ndyomugenyi (I'm a visitor), followed by Butariko whose name refers to the season when sorghum flowers bloom. Butariko didn't live to see his sixth birthday. Baakataaka (crafted like a beautiful decorative basket), was the first daughter, and after her, Batomi (as small as a fist, the result of probable premature birth). Nyabuzaana suffered two devastating miscarriages before I came along, remembered with grief by Baakataaka. Right on my heels, Ntwiga (beautiful like a zebra) was born.

Our family is part of a proud clan called the Baheesi, part of a larger group, the Bakiga. Within our tribe we maintain strong clan associations that dictate cultural norms surrounding marriage, burial, and naming children. A famous saying in our part of the world: A person without a clan is like a tree without roots, easily uprooted or felled by insignificant weather My father, Mutana, whose name literally means "quiver" - like a quiver full of arrows - is the son of a lengthy line of proud Baheesi. At Mutana's birth, a friend gave Mutambuka an actual arrow, a symbolic gift to mark the expansion of his family.

Like arrows in the hands of a warrior are children born in one's youth. Blessed is the man whose quiver is full of them.

- Psalm 127:4-5

This is my lineage, seven generations before me.
I am Mugarura,

son of Mutana,

son of Mutambuka,

son of Rutogogo,

son of Ncuro of Kyomya,

son of Bebwa,

son of Shumbusho,

son of Katozo.

The Baheesi have claimed Bukoora as their ancestral home, but history tells us they moved there from Ruhengyere. They moved from Ruhengyere to Mugyera and Rubaya, and were settled in Bukoora by my grandfather, Mutambuka.

Mutambuka is a larger-than-life character in the story of our clan, and speaking his name inevitably generates fanciful tales, some based in history and others creative works of fiction, certain to entertain for hours. His nickname is Runyasi rwa Nguga orutararira nju ya mworo. This fanciful title signified that he considered himself as dangerous as "Nguga" - a special tall grass that hides among other grasses and grows at high altitudes. Its razor-sharp edges can slice soft human skin open.

"Orutararira nju ya mworo" means "the one who does not stay in the house of a poor person". When he visited, he expected the family to slaughter a goat for dinner, a difficulty for poor families. As a skilled, respected and often consulted herbalist, people travelled from far-flung places to get remedies for all manner of illnesses. He wielded extraordinary spiritual powers called emandwa which, when malevolent, were capable of incredible evil, and conversely resulted in astonishing goodness, giving him a position of immense power in his corner of the World. Seeing him walk up to your door for a visit was an enormous deal.

The Bakiga settled in Kigezi, a high-altitude area of south-western Uganda close to the border with Rwanda and the Democratic Republic of the Congo. Prior to colonialism, powerful and expansionist kingdoms surrounded them, their conflicts often ensnaring sections of the population. In the gaps between the kingdoms, shimmering lakes and rushing rivers too dangerous to cross hemmed them in, natural barriers which are part of the geographical features of the Great Rift Valley. As the population grew, requiring bigger chunks of land for agriculture and livestock, the region erupted into full-blown conflict, and they battled each other to defend or expand their territories.

The strife lasted for the better part of the 19th century, stealing countless lives, leaving bereaved families who nursed roiling vengeance in their hearts, and complicating hostilities between the clans. During this turbulent time, the Baheesi roamed with their families through the rough terrain, looking for defensible positions and forging alliances with other clans.

Mutambuka began by moving his people from Mugyera to Rubaya where, to this day, there remains a site referred to as eitongo rya Mutambuka meaning, "Mutambuka's former homestead". After a few years in Rubaya, he led them to a steep, imposing hill called Bukoora. From this hill he could overlook the surrounding area, giving him a strategic military advantage.

In the lore of our clan, my grandfather is elevated almost to god-like status. Not just because he established our ancestral home in Bukoora, but because he found ingenious ways to defend his family from the ravages of war.

One story features prominently in my mind; When Katuregye son of Kanaganago turned his greedy gaze towards Bukoora.

In the late 19th Century, King Rwabugiri of Rwanda led three invasions against clans in the northern part of present day Rwanda, and south-west Uganda. Thousands of displaced people migrated north into Kigezi, former elites usurped traditional landholders and grabbed their property. Displaced people roamed the mountains, homeless and hungry, intensifying the conflict; a powder keg ready to explode.

The disruption to people's lives meant agriculture came to a complete standstill, rampant livestock raiding was the order of the day, and finally in 1895 and again in 1905 a severe famine ravaged the population, each one lasting at least three years. Rinderpest swept through the livestock, reducing vast herds to a ragged collection of malnourished animals unable to sustain the lives Bakiga once knew.

This devastation created the perfect storm for vicious warlords, including Basebye, Muhumuza, and Katuregye, who rose to prominence as they conquered people and land for their survival and greed.

Sitting atop the Bakongwe clan, Katuregye subjugated and absorbed forty clans. Facing defeat, many clans made a choice for peace, giving him the most beautiful of their daughters for wives, hoping it cemented a familial relationship, making future conflict impossible.

Katuregye's army was a collection of ferocious mercenaries from a reclusive and mysterious pygmy tribe from the mountains called the Batwa. Their skill with the bow and arrow meant they didn't have to meet the much larger Bakiga in hand-to-hand combat. They advanced east, cutting down hundreds of warriors before them and razing them to the ground, until they got to Bukoora, Mutambuka's fortified home in the hills.

A place straight out of the imagination of fantasy writers, Bukoora perches on a steep, dominant peak on one of the parallel ranges that eventually rise to form the Rwenzori Mountain. It is covered in a thick blanket of lush life that hides a block of crystalline rocks raised by the underlying tectonic plates. Soil erosion carved out gaping caves all over Bukoora, and the perpetual split of the African plate formed the Great Rift Valley, Muhabura Mountain, and Rwenzori Mountain. It is still an area of high tectonic and volcanic activity. One of the deepest lakes in the world, Lake Bunyonyi, is a crater lake on the western slopes of Bukoora. Mutambuka's home was a sparkling jewel, a temptation for the warrior audacious enough to pluck it from the leaders.

The elevation of Mutambuka's home in Bukoora gave him a strategic vantage point, allowing him to see across Lake Bunyonyi for threats from neighbouring tribes. Spying the trunk-carved boats overflowing with Katuregye's brutal warriors cresting over the horizon, Mutambuka hid his family in Katwaro cave, a massive hole nature gouged out of the mountain on the eastern slope of the hill. He was not keen on engaging in direct combat.

Katuregye arrived to find empty homes, abandoned hearths, and a dearth of livestock he could claim for himself. They looted and ransacked homes, emptying granaries, and took as much food and livestock as they could carry. Boats loaded to capacity, they sailed back to their camp on the western shores of Lake Bunyonyi.

Loaded with free spoils from people too cowardly to meet them in battle, Katuregye ordered the sacrifice of the largest bull to the gods of his clan.

Katuregye either hadn't heard of Mutambuka or didn't believe the stories he'd heard, otherwise he wouldn't have taken the property of the most powerful sorcerer of his time. Mutambuka had protected his animals with a potent spell.

Katuregye's warriors got their knives ready and approached Mutambuka's prized bull, Rushokangondo, chief of the herd, eager for the sacrifice. Every single person who dared to cut Rushokangondo's skin gasped in pain from mysterious stab wounds that cut deep into their flesh. After several attempts from brave warriors who'd watched their comrades scream in pain, and urgent queries from surrounding clans, Katuregye discovered whose homestead he'd attacked. He assembled a delegation who flew over the lake with great haste to plead with Mutambuka and beg for his forgiveness. Mutambuka agreed on condition that the Bakongwe return everything they'd stolen and cease their attack on the Baheesi. Terrified and prostrate, Katuregye complied, offering three girls to Mutambuka as wives and sealing a peace pact between the two clans.

He never attacked the Baheesi again, but the heartbeat of war thrummed in his chest, too loud to ignore, and he continued his expansionist ambitions. Embroiled in a civil war over the succession of King Rwabugiri, Katuregye, allied with Biregeya, Rwabugiri's son by the notorious rebel and freedom fighter, Queen Muhumuza. The fight for the throne ensnared German and British colonialists who fought for the other son, Musinga, who'd claimed the throne. In one of these battles against the colonial forces, Katuregye met his end, his dreams of spreading his influence in Kigezi dissipating with his defeated forces.

My father's history weaves through this rich tapestry, a thread of would-be coincidences choke-full of evidence that God was preparing my path, placing me in a fascinating family.

At the time of his death, Mutambuka had over thirty wives who bore him multiple children. One of his first wives came from the Basigyi of Omukirwa, Muruhita. Her parents named her Bwandungi. Mutana was their eldest son, and Nyakarasi their second.

Being romantic at heart, Bakiga men give their wives names of endearment. They don't abandon or forget their original names, but the family they've married into, use the wife-name. Mutambuka named Bwandungi, Keiriza (her beauty makes men shed tears of admiration and desire). When he got married, Mutana named Nyabuzaana, Kenyanje (as beautiful and graceful as an egret). I kept that tradition when I married Joyie (curb your curiosity, you'll find out the name I gave her soon enough), and so did my son, Paul, who named his wife Karungi.

The Bakiga did not adopt the Gregorian calendar until decades after my father's birth, and aside from dates marked by royal births in neighbouring tribes, no one recorded other births in the same manner. Instead, stories surrounding birth soar on the wings of a strong oral tradition, and get passed around with great exuberance. As with all oral traditions, a thread of truth binds the story together even when the details have become somewhat fuzzy. Unfortunately, it means we do not know the date of my father's birth.

We know that Mutana's birth happened around the time of tremendous geopolitical change in Africa, when colonial powers descended on the continent, carving out pieces for economic benefit. They fought each other by entrapping desperate leaders and drawing them into wars against other African leaders who resisted conquest. Germans, Portuguese, French, and British forces swarmed the land, claiming large swaths as protectorates and installing themselves as colonialists. Uganda was a protectorate of the British Empire, and they entrenched their rule through Christian religion. Preceding the colonisers, British missionaries promoted Anglicanism, and they evangelised my grandfather and his entire family, converting them from the animistic religion they'd embraced for generations.

Mutambuka's baptism happened a few weeks before his death, and he followed the rule the missionaries instituted, giving himself a Western/Biblical name to signify the change in religion. He chose the name Mark (Marko among the Bakiga). This seed of Christianity stayed in the family, flourishing long after Mutambuka's death.

My father and uncle followed in their father's footsteps and got baptized too. Mutana took the name Blasio (Blaise), and Nyakarasi chose Yokana (John). Through the teachings of the church, Mutana became a devoted Christian, which led to his appointment as a church teacher. He planted a church in Nyabitabo near Kaharo on the Kabale - Mbarara road. The church still exists today.

Blasio Mutana came of age and decided it was time to get married. In Butare, a village in the shadow of Kitumba hill, he met a tall, slender girl and desired her for a wife. Her father, Katutu (son of Bigyenda of the Bariisa clan) had lived a tumultuous life, first as a herdsman, then as an abductee in the Kingdom of Rwanda, and finally as an escapee and refugee, a lost boy amongst strangers. Katutu was a casualty of the clan wars in the mid-to-late 19th Century, kidnapped when cattle rustlers stole livestock as part of their spoils of war. Even after a daring escape from his captors, he failed to find his way back to his people, and ended up being absorbed in a Hima clan called Abanyonyi. Katutu married a woman weighed down with her own trauma from the loss of her entire family (a husband and two sons) to the famine that swept East Africa, taking millions of lives as it went. They had four daughters, Nyabuzaana, Karuuku, Karibara, and Bakesiima.

Once the elders of the Baheesi approved of his choice, my father married Nyabuzaana (Kenyanje) and she converted to Christianity, baptized as Tofasi Margaret. Her parents gave them a cow to start their own herd, one they knew would produce calves. In the absence of monetary currency, cows symbolized wealth and were a particularly prized possession. Not only were they used to pay for large transactions, they were the most essential part of the bride price. Even if your other gifts were many ebishebo (gifts), with elaborate emikyeka (mats), delicately woven ebyibio (baskets), or large ebitukuru and enyungu (pots), they'd amount to nothing without the presentation of cows. Many cows.

The cow gifted to Nyabuzaana was a backdoor way of ensuring wealth followed their daughter into the family she was about to join.

It turned out to be very fertile, producing many other calves for the herd. When Mutana was ready to increase the size of the family by marrying a third, then later a fourth wife, he asked Nyabuzaana's permission for the offspring her cow had spawned, using them as part of the bride price for his new wives. Years later, when my eldest brother, Ndyomugenyi, was getting married, he used cattle descended from Nyabuzaana's cow.

In the polygamous tradition of his forefathers, Mutana married four different women. Nyabuzaana was his first wife, and Karibara (Nyabuzaana's younger sister) was his second. Mutana gave Karibara the endearment name, Bashemera. Nyirabagisha became the third wife, who Mutana called Bakuundwa, and Ruth Keishemura was his fourth and last wife.

I am my parent's fifth child, born in Kitumba sub-county, which was a part of Ndorwa county in Bukoora, outside Kabale city in South West Uganda.

My father wrote our birth dates on the inside of an ancient wooden trunk, making the handwriting difficult to read. Truthfully, I am not sure which day or year I was born, but according to my family it was the 9th or the 13th of October. When I was being registered for school, there was confusion about my date of birth and the year I was born, so I arbitrarily chose 9th October as my birthday, and 1941 as the year in which I was born.

When I was born, they gave me the name Mugarura. I omitted the lengthy story behind the meaning of my name when I talked about my siblings' names, and the events surrounding their birth. Are you ready?

The Bakiga name children according to the prevailing circumstances around their birth. For example, if a boy is born at night his parents might choose the name Bwanyekiro, "He came at night". Or if a girl is born during the rainy season, she might have the name Nyanjura which means, "She was born during the rainfall." If a child was born during war times, he or she would be Rutaro, which literally means "war". If there were conflicts between co-wives, relatives, or neighbours, they would name the children born during that conflict "Muzarirehe" to ask where a child should be born. If a mother had lost several children, they would give the child born after the losses an awful name like Babinuga hoping death would avoid the child, believing that the anthropomorphized "Death" disliked taking children with terrible names.

While Nyabuzaana was pregnant with me, she had a fight with Mutana and left for her parents' home. However, Mutambuka had decreed that any male child born outside his father's home would die unless he they brought him back immediately. Mutambuka's words carried particular gravitas as a priest of Nyabinghi, wielding mysterious spiritual powers known by the Bakiga as emandwa, and no one who knew him dared challenge his declarations. The moment I was born, there was an understandable flurry of activity to return me to Mutana's home, especially because I followed two heartbreaking miscarriages.

The word "return" in Rukiga is "okugarura". The baby and his mother had to be okugarurwa. Under normal circumstances, they followed a particular process. The wife's family would convene a court of elders and hear from the man and his wife, making a judgement according to tradition and all the evidence presented. If they needed more information, the husband could bring representation from his family, and any evidence he might have. If they found him guilty of having caused his wife's departure, they'd fine him, paid fully in one goat.

However, in my parents' case, there was an extra sense of urgency, and to avoid Mutambuka's curse they rushed me back home, and my grandmother, as a result, named me "Akaamugarwire" (they returned him) later shortened to "Mugarura".

Something that only occurred to me later in life is that the name my grandmother gave me has a prophetic dimension to it. She was not a Christian, and at the time she was just giving me a name based on the circumstances of my birth. But when I finally made a commitment to serve Jesus with my life, God used me to return people to him. It has been the joy of my life to bring people back into relationship with God. So my name has more significance than just being a marker of the return of a child. It was also a word spoken into my life that I would be a part of "okugarura" - returning people to God.

In the late 1930s to early 40s, my parents were peasants who tilled the land and kept livestock, but otherwise had no other source of income. Through a series of unfortunate events and terrible misunderstanding, Mutana fell out of favour with the leadership of the Anglican church.

As one of the few, and earliest people educated among the Bakiga, Mutana had risen through the ranks of leadership and was well on his way to a bright future which didn't sit well with some who watched his meteoric rise. With malice in their hearts, they placed witchcraft somewhere along his path to curtail his success, and he stepped over it, oblivious to the danger.

By the time he reached Nyabitabo, sickness had gripped his body, an invisible chain dragging him to death's door so he couldn't return home. Puzzled and alarmed, the people at the church rushed him to Rugarama Hospital in Kabale, bouncing him along on engazi, a portable bed, and the hospital staff admitted him with haste. Days passed, his condition worsening by the hour, perplexed doctors hovering over his bed, holding test results that didn't explain his sudden sickness.

Word reached Mutambuka that his son was dying, surrounded by people unable to cure him, so he hastened two of his sons to the hospital. Mutana's condition was dire, and they whisked him out of the hospital and sped to Mutambuka's side. Mutambuka diagnosed the problem and began essential treatment to save Mutana's life, which included a combination of traditional medicine and spiritual care using emandwa.

When the increasingly conservative leadership heard that Mutambuka used emandwa to save Mutana's life, they erupted in anger, accusing Mutana of indulging in witchcraft which, in their opinion, was in direct conflict with the values of Christianity.

On another occasion, a senior member of Church leadership visited our family home. Like many other cultures, the Bakiga offer refreshments to visitors who've travelled long distances. My mother served fresh omuramba (alcohol) to the church leader, believing she was honoring his presence in our home. This added insult to an already festering wound, and the leader declared that Mutana and Nyabuzaana had gone too far. They ostracized Mutana and stripped him of leadership of the congregation he planted.

It was during this tumultuous time that I came screaming into the World. With the loss of standing in the church, my parents could not baptize me, an important tradition in the Anglican Church. At the baptism ceremony the parents of an infant choose a name, typically Western or Biblical, that goes along with the traditional name marking the occasion of their birth. Later on in my story, this will explain why

I chose a name of my own.

Being resourceful and educated, after Mutana left the church he landed a cushy administrative job as Muluka chief with the colonial government, but it took him from Bukoora all the way to Karujanga, almost eighty kilometers away. He became the head of the local government, a post created by the colonialists who'd chopped up the country into provinces, small counties, and even smaller sub-counties, appointing local people as chiefs and administrators. Gombolola chiefs administered counties, and Muluka chiefs, sub-counties.

Mutana's job took us away from the extended family in Bukoora, stretching relationships between us almost to the point of breaking. The responsibility of raising a mukiga child was not the purview of the parents alone. The entire community took part. Most people lived with their clan members for the bulk of their lives, having no way to travel to distant places. Relatives and neighbours occupied similar positions of cultural authority over children in the community, often disciplining wayward children and teaching them the cultural norms and traditions of the Bakiga.

Older generations folded the young under their wings, passing on oral tradition, teaching dignity and respect, training them in traditional farming practices, singing songs bursting with the history of their people, and celebrating their culture through poetry. The responsibility of making girls into dutiful wives fell to grandmothers and aunts, while uncles and grandfathers made sure the boys knew how to build strong, long-lasting homes. Being separated from the larger family was strange, difficult even, but we all bore it with grace, understanding the sacrifice our parents were making on our behalf.

In Karujanga, the lay leadership of the local church operated the primary school and didn't have full accreditation from the government. The founding lay church leaders had learned to read and write from missionaries, the first wave of Europeans to arrive in Central Africa. The Bible was the only available written text, and missionaries used it to teach literacy to the Bakiga. This is how Mutana became literate.

The Omushomesa (teacher) was the leader of the church and occupied many teaching roles in the community. He led weekly worship services, preached whenever there was a need, and taught congregants about the Bible. He taught catechist classes to people seeking conversion through baptism, and conducted literacy classes for the community. Parents like mine, keen on having literate children, sent them to makeshift church schools.

Set in a money-poor community, and unfunded by the government, our school did not have paper, books, pencils, multiple chalkboards, or chalk. We sat in rows in the dust, and smoothed the spaces between the rows, where we practiced writing numbers and letters by tracing them with our fingers. If Omushomesa came and found your numbers or words lacking, he'd erase your work with a simple swipe of his foot.

Clothing made from woven cotton was scarce, a commodity purchased using money that most of the community did not have. It was expensive and considered a luxury, so we all dressed the same. The boys in my class wore a goat skin draped over one shoulder, the front legs sewn together with string; an informal uniform for the school. If a football game got started after school, or a running competition got sparked by male bravado, we'd toss the skins over willing friends' arms and run around nude. The chaffing of dried goat skin against soft human skin is an unbearable uniform for sporting activities, so no one considered our collective nudity offensive or sexual.

Our patriarchal society possessed strict rules and regulations regarding the roles of girls/women and boys/men. They confined girls and women to tasks inside the house, although boys collected firewood, taking care of the livestock in families wealthy enough to own animals, and bringing water home from the community well. Some girls had no brothers, which meant herding livestock was their responsibility. When other boys discovered girls in their midst, they took it upon themselves to tease them mercilessly because they were performing tasks outside the house. Men's things.

In education, the same opinions kept girls away from school, instead preferring that they stay home doing chores and assisting their mothers. This made my sisters ineligible for church school. Bakataaka only made it to primary four, Batomi had no formal education, and Ntwiga didn't make it past primary six.

Church school started at eight o'clock in the morning, going on till one in the afternoon. My brother, Katungi (from my father's second wife, Karibara), and I would race home every day after school, our stomach rumbling with hunger and the exertion of educating our young minds. The school and church coffers were too empty to afford a snack or lunch, and we salivated at the thought of the yummy smells that would hit us as we walked through the doors of our home. Like other children at that age, the hunger gnawing inside wasn't enough to drag us straight home, so we'd entertain ourselves with a game we'd invented; throwing stones at birds to see if we could hit them.

I went to the church school in Karujanga for a year, then transferred to another church school in Kibuga, further away from our home. When that school year ended, it was time for me to take a qualification exam to go to the sub-grade school in Kamuganguzi.

Church schools from the entire region joined in this high stakes competition to find the thirty-five smartest kids to send to this highly prized school.

That day is etched into my mind. The chilly morning that didn't climb out of the single digits, every muscle quivering to warm me up. The lengthy line of eager, nervous kids, half listening to important instructions for the exam. We gazed through the windows of the buildings at Kamuganguzi and envisioned ourselves learning about the fantastic world. They divided us into groups, giving each one a slate with writing lines already marked on it, along with a slate pencil. Some students of the school looked at this ragtag collection of unsophisticated kids, draped in animal skin and acted upon their prejudice. While the elders' attention was away from us, they took our slate boards and pencils, exchanging them for white boards and chalk.

The enormous examination room swallowed our shivering bodies, and at the front of the examination room, the teacher wrote questions on the blackboards, instructing us to write our answers on the slates they'd given us. At the end of the exam, I watched my slate disappear under the pile of other slates the teacher gathered for grading, my heart pounding in my ears. It was such an intimidating experience that to this day I cannot explain how I passed the examination to snag one of the thirty-five spots. I'd never held a writing slate, nor handled pencil or dusty chalk whose residue clung to my hands.

For two years, primary three and four, I stayed at Kamuganguzi Primary School, much to the envy of throngs of kids who'd failed the exam. In primary five I transferred to Kikungiri Primary School, perched on the outskirts of Kabale town. The daily trek to Karujanga was too far for me, but thankfully it was closer to our family home in Bukoora, and I got to stay with my maternal grandmother.

Even though Bukoora is closer to Kikungiri Primary School than Karujanga is, it was still a long walk for a young boy. I'd leave close to dawn when the chittering baby birds woke their parents from sleep, and would come home with just enough time to enjoy the final few minutes of daylight before my grandmother sent me off to bed. For two whole years I saw very little of my family in Karujanga, or my extended family in Bukoora, with one exception. My paternal uncle, Kosia Miranda.

Kosia was a builder, but ended up a Muluka chief just like Mutana, because he was literate. In those days, he had the greatest impact on my young life. We'd walk home together at the end of the workday, me from school and him from work, chatting about everything, and anything, and nothing. Possessed with a flair for exaggeration, he'd concoct incredible tales that had me rolling in stitches, or gasping at vivid horrors. He embellished stories to distract me from our long journey home, keeping me entertained. With his larger-than-life personality, he chose a nickname for himself. Staffingi Raddar Nyarubabi. The entire family found it hilarious and stacked it like a title in front of his name, and thus he became Staffingi Raddar Nyarubabi Kosia Miranda.

He was my favourite person, showing me the ways of the world. Uncle Kosia taught me how to build a house, filled in the gaps of the history of the Baheesi, taught me life lessons that I carried in my heart for a long time. He was the father figure I needed during those years of intense development when I lived with my grandmother.

When I enrolled in Kikungiri Primary School, I thought I was like everybody else. We spoke the same language, came from similar economic backgrounds, none of us wore shoes. Something still bothered me. Where they had two or three names, foreign and heavy on the tongue, I only had one. While it's true that the Bakiga gave one name at birth, Christianity changed the game and multiplied the number of names. It hadn't bothered me that my name was Mugarura, son of Mutana, son of Mutambuka, and so on, but this difference was a gaping hole that, despite my efforts to ignore, blinked and jangled in my mind, making me feel odd and out of place.

Being the resourceful child I was, I joined the catechist class of 1955 in Kikungiri to recruit new converts. This was where I'd get a new name and finally be the same as everyone else. With my parents back in Karujanga, too far for proper consultation, I chose my name. They required a Christian name for conversion, so the Bible was the obvious source of baptismal names. There was a dearth to choose from, some that schoolmates rallied for, but when I read the name Benoni in Genesis 35:18, the youngest son of Jacob, I knew I'd found what I was searching for. It sounded cool and no one else had the smarts to find such a cool name, so it was now mine and I relished in my choice. I didn't bother with research to find out what it meant.

The trendy thing to do at baptism in 1955 was to have two Western/Christian names. John Pauls, Simon Peter, and Jane Frances ran rampant in Kabale. Many of my schoolmates chose the name John, and being a contrarian who sought uniqueness, I chose Jack. The joke was on me, however, because I later found out that Jack is the diminutive of the name John.

Benoni held a special place in my heart, becoming the name I used when I introduced myself. It stuck! My full name is Benoni Jack Mugarura-Mutana.

My father's second wife is my mother's younger sister, Karibara. Relationships between children born in polygamous families are challenging, but relationships between children of sisters bound to the same man through marriage have the potential to be explosive. Despite that, I have a special relationship with my half-brother, Samuel Baker Katungi, the firstborn of Karibara. Katungi is only a few months older than I, and even now we look like twins and everyone treated us like twins.

From time to time, as he performed his Muluka chief duties, my father took Katungi and me along with him. We watched him with awe as he arbitrated conflicts in the community, wielding his wisdom to subdue irate neighbours, or couples, or business partners. In between administrative work and arbitrations, he'd ask us to sing the songs we'd learned at school. In his playful way, he'd replace some words with nonsensical phrases of his own, turning boring English songs into Rukiga with subtle but hilarious meaning. We laughed and repeated these songs whenever we could, at school and at home.

Marrying a second wife wasn't the move a repentant Christian seeking the approval of church leaders would take. His standing as a church leader had already suffered a fatal blow, but polygamy was deeply ingrained in the lives of the Bakiga, increasing their families and their wealth. Even with deeply wounding commentary on his life, and stolen disapproving glances from the leadership, my devout father continued to attend church services, sitting on the chair my brother and I carried for him. The church had no seats, and respectable members of society didn't sit on the floor with women and children and unmarried men. It was a gentleman's responsibility to bring his own chair to church.

My father would urge us on, his long strides taking us faster than our little legs could take us, and we'd arrive way before the service started. The call to confession and repentance is a part of the opening penitential rite in the 1662 order of Anglican liturgy, a fact I'd later find out when I attended seminary. Mutana referred to it as "When a wicked man turns away from his wickedness."

Mutana was not conservative as one might think, considering his devotion to a church that had rejected him and his way of life. On one hand, he was a stereotypical African patriarch commanding the respect of the family and the clan, using it to keep peace and order amongst four wives and many children. His penchant for fun, his approach to affectionate parenting, and openness drew us close to him. Katungi and I often sought him out and stuck as close as possible to him as he walked through the community, ran beside him as he walked to church, or lurked close by when he was home during his free time. He overflowed with fables meant to guide our morality, comedies that had us clutching our tummies and rolling on the floor, or serious tales about ancestors doing miraculous things. He had a flair for the dramatic, which sharpened the images in our minds, keeping all of us enraptured. It's a feature that found its way down the line, through me and my siblings, to our children, keeping us entertained with dramatic embellishments, and uproarious stories.

Work and church were not the only places my father took us. Whenever a male child was born into the family, they placed omuramba on the child's lips, the parents believing that a tolerance for the beverage would make the child strong. Following my father to makeshift bars run out of different homes was no issue at all. As expected, fights broke out between drunk men, destroying property and hurting themselves and even sometimes onlookers. Lawsuits and demands for retribution would inevitably find their way to my father's arbitration court. As a way to curry favour from him they made sure the chief had a steady flow of drink at the bar and even at home, hoping that if they ever had to bring a case to him, he'd make a judgement in their favour. That's how Katungi and I had easy access to copious amounts of omuramba. It wasn't saved just for the adults, children got to enjoy it, and my father never made a big deal out of seeing us tipsy. It doesn't take a giant leap to see how it led me into alcohol addiction at a young age, engulfing years of my youth. I stumbled around in a drunken stupor, stuck in a rut that should have ended in my death, while other lives flourished around me.

2

Unlikely Start

January 1961 rolled around, bringing one of the most exciting journeys of my life, something I'd dreamed about and worked hard for. I was going to Siniya, Kigezi College Butobere. The boys of that esteemed school strutted through the streets of Kabale draped in bright blue sweaters, long khaki Stockport shorts, rain capes billowing behind them. Through my years at Kikungiri Primary School, every exam I did, every time I studied instead of playing with my friends, was to get accepted at Siniya.

My mother and I went shopping for all the things a senior one boy required; bedsheets, a towel, khaki shorts, a white, short-sleeved, button-down shirt, and spare clothes. We packed them into a wooden box that served as my suitcase. Proper ones were far beyond our meagre budget, and in the crisp, chilly morning air I donned my uniform, wore my brand new black plastic shoes and started my journey to Siniya.

Three kilometers from our house to the bus stop, one bus ride to the T-junction on Katuna road, and the muscle-exhausting walk to the College campus later, I arrived at the gates of my dream secondary school. The wood box balanced on my freshly shaved head should have bothered me, but excitement painted the experience with a brush that glowed with expectations for a bright future. Nothing could bring me down that day.

Kabale, the Switzerland of Africa, is a bustling town snuggled in the steep hills of Kigezi, and is 2,000 metres (6,600 feet) above sea level. The elevation of some hills rise above a dizzying 3,500 metres, turning a walk in any direction into a climb up a steep hill. The walk from the bus park to Siniya is one of the steepest.

I'd visited Siniya before, so I knew the effort it would take to get there, but with the weight of the wood box on my head and neck and shoulders, and the uncomfortable Sandak shoes from Bata (a luxury few people could afford), my discomfort might have made the journey difficult. When I got to the gate I was exhausted, sunburnt, and growing multiple blisters on my heels, but my spirit soared with my dreams as my eyes drew in my new school. I made it!

Like a spider leaving the tangle of its nest, the gatekeeper's long arms and legs stretched from the shelter beside the school gate. He stretched out a tall body, casting a dark shadow that covered my entire body. He slapped a truncheon in his palm; a warning for trespassers.

"What is your name?" He'd probably said it a dozen times before I'd gotten there.

I stuck my chest out and raised my voice. I was a Siniya boy, after all. "Benoni Mugarura."

Before the gatekeeper could respond, someone I couldn't see called out loud and clear, "You can't be Mugarura. We already have one here."

A smart alec who came to tease the new boy, the first of many attempts he'd make. Stephen Tumushabe was a year ahead of me, and for reasons I cannot explain to this day, laying his eyes on me made him want to frustrate my efforts into settling in school. Thankfully, some other student was passing by, saw the puzzled look on my face, and helped the new kid find his dormitory, Makobore House, and together we carried my wood box to my room.

The common hazing practice involved making new students take a cold shower with the frigid water of the mountains. Stephen took another swipe at me and came to my dorm room, shook me from the deepest slumber, dragged my exhausted, groggy body to the bathroom, and ordered me to shower. He'd grown up in the lower elevation of Kigezi, in Kambuga, and didn't know I'd taken cold showers at the top of the mountain in Bukora, a mainstay of our grooming regimen. He listened with growing horror as I whistled and sang, enjoying the magic of indoor plumbing absent in Bukoora, and washed away the long bus ride, heavy luggage, and sweat of the climb to the school. Stephen barged into the showers, yelling about wasting water and taking too long, shouting a slur used to insult newcomers. "Bigata! Bigata! Bigata!"

I sauntered out of the shower with my brand new towel wrapped around my waist. He reached up and ran rough hands through my hair, checking to make sure I'd stood under the water. With a wry look of defeat on his face, he ordered me to get dressed and sent me back to my room, but didn't tease me again. A few weeks after that we were fast friends. Where you found one of us, the other lurked close by.

A year later, I inherited a bicycle from Ndyomugenyi that I used to ride around Kabale. Stephen was a week late for school, but sent a message to let me know when he'd be arriving at the bus stop. The bus ride from Kambuga was much further than Bukoora, and I knew Stephen would be tired, plus it was a chance to see my best friend after a long holiday.

I found a weakness in the school's perimeter and slipped through it, riding down the rough stone road to the bus stop. The skip and lurch of my heart interrupted my enthusiastic wave when I saw who followed him; a beautiful, petite, light-skinned girl, who floated on clouds and out of a bus I suddenly wished I'd been on.

My tongue and brain disconnected, words became meaningless, and I kept my mouth closed till I could think of something clever to say. As we waited for the conductor to unstrap and lower their cases from the top of the bus, Stephen introduced me to his younger sister, Topher Joyie Tumwijuke Turahi.

My mind raced as I racked my brain for a quick plan that would allow me to spend every spare second in this magnificent creature's presence. I came up with one that was brilliant, if I say so myself.

Joyie enrolled at Kabale Girls Junior Secondary School in Rwere. The road to Joyie's school stretched up Rugarama hill, and past Kigezi High School, a bitter rival of Siniya. They believed that the girls from Rwere preferred the boys at Siniya and perched themselves along the school fence to harass the poor girls as they walked by.

Her case was the same size as Stephen's even though she was less than half his size. I convinced them both that it would be prudent and chivalrous to make sure she got to school without embarrassment. Stephen reluctantly agreed, strapped his case to my bicycle, and I hefted Joyie's on my head. I barely noticed the heckling boys at Kigezi High as we walked past, immersed in the conversation about... to this day, I cannot remember. By the time we got to Rwere's gates, passed her the suitcase, and watched her walk off, dust from the road powdered on the back of her calves, I was smitten.

I could not get her out of my mind, and kept replaying our time together, thinking how intelligent she was in keeping the conversation engaging. I yearned to stay in contact with her, so I wrote her a note, but getting the note to her was a near-impossible task.

English missionaries dedicated to safeguarding the innocence, and virtue of the girls ran Kabale Girls Junior Secondary School. Even contact with their own parents was difficult, so there was little hope for love-struck boys like me, minds swarming with less virtuous thoughts, to have even the briefest contact with them.

But young hearts will find a way. A distant relative worked as a gatekeeper at Siniya, and had a home in Rwere, near Kabale Girls. I begged and pleaded with him to take a note to one girl at the school, and seeing my desperation, he agreed to do it. I took a page out of one of my notebooks, wrote a brief letter to her, and sent it with him, and after a few days, it overjoyed me to receive a note back. With our lines of communication established, we started sending frequent notes to each other, each one getting longer and longer. We talked a lot about the next time we would see each other, and there were two opportunities. The first was at the weekly English service at the Anglican cathedral in Rugarama, and the second was at the schools' sports day held at the Kabale stadium.

The weekly English service at Rugarama cathedral was in the afternoon, and the boys of Siniya packed themselves into the school lorry and took the five kilometer trip to church. The girls from Rwere walked to the cathedral, which was closer to their school, arranged in long lines with teachers leading the troupe, and others guarding the middle and the back. We often remarked that they were being herded like sheep.

Reverend Richard Lyth, the first Bishop of Kigezi Diocese, was the provost. I enjoyed going to the services because he was engaging and did most of the preaching. However, after I met Joyie, all I wanted to do was catch a glimpse of her, barely hearing the messages from the pulpit. During the services, the best we could do with the girls was steal glances at each other. If we waved to them and they dared to wave back, their missionary teachers would swiftly reprimand them. We satisfied ourselves with nods, glances, or other surreptitious hand signals.

Our next best option, the schools' sports day at the stadium, was not much better than the cathedral. The same long lines with hawk-eyed teachers shepherded the girls to a corner of the stadium, far from the students of all other participating schools. They were only let out of the corner during races they competed in.

Topher was one of the fastest sprinters in her division, coming in first or second in short-distance races and hurdles. Being neither gifted in sprinting nor really any other sport, Stephen was my frequent excuse for showing up in the stadium. Like his sister, he was a fast sprinter, often winning middle distance races.

During the races I'd cheer till my voice was hoarse, hoping she'd hear me yelling her name. As the teachers herded them out of the stadium, I would haunt a strategic vantage point from which we'd catch each other's eyes and wave as they left in their perfect lines. Once they disappeared around the corner, I'd run back to the parked school lorry, pleased and disappointed, and filled with all the confusion of a teenager falling in love.

One day the letters stopped coming and my mind filled with all the possibilities, each of them ending in separation from the object of my affections. Unbeknownst to me, a routine end-of-term check had uncovered letters filled with all the yearnings of teen love, and promptly mailed to her father.

Samwiri Turahi was a strict conservative Christian leader in his community, and not about to abandon his daughter to the pinnings of a school boy. He grilled her about me, how she met me and developed a friendship to the extent that romantic letters were being shipped back and forth from her school to his.

Explaining that she'd met me through Stephen seemed to make things a little better, but he let her off with strict instructions to conduct herself with more dignity around teenage boys.

Samwiri Turahi was unique, urging his children to invite their friends home so he and their mother could get to know them. It was their way of examining the personalities and behavior of the people their children hung out with, making sure they had a beneficial influence on them.

That's how I got to visit Kambuga for the first time. Stephen invited me to their home, just a friend from Siniya coming to visit, and the real motive - visiting Topher without raising suspicion from their parents - remained hidden from them for many years.

Circa 1965-66, Kabale, Uganda.

3

Unlikely Future

By the time I started my first year in Siniya, I was a blossoming alcoholic. I was also a haughty young man who refused to follow rules created by people I didn't respect. Coupled with the foolishness and immaturity of youth, I convinced myself that no rules applied to me, whether they were temporal or divine. Proud of my rebellious nature, I believed I could do anything and get away with it.

I figured out ways to break school rules without being found out. After lights out, I snuck off the school campus to one of the local bars, which sold omuramba. I'd buy some and bring it to school to share with other students who shared my taste for it. The more I broke the rules and got away with it, the more brazen I became, each daring feat cheered on by my peers and further fueled by my addiction.

As you would expect, this kind of behaviour led to a decline in my academics. The boy who worked so hard to get to Siniya, and celebrated the acceptance into this coveted school, found himself routinely at the bottom of the class after every end of term examination.

In senior three, they elected me as to student leadership. The position I ran for and got was the entertainment minister, responsible for organizing extra-curricular entertainment. My profile as a smuggler of omuramba into the school helped boost my student leadership campaign. I used my position as a student leader to instigate a sit-down strike that started in the first term of my third year in Siniya.

During the three years I was at Siniya, we had seen one science teacher after another arrive at the school, teach for a little while, and then leave, either returning to Kampala or going to other schools like Nyakasura. Except for our headmaster, a brilliant math teacher, we had limited science instruction and there was growing discontent among the students.

At the end of the first four years of secondary school in Uganda, students sit a national exam (today known as the Uganda Certificate of Education, or UCE), and there are four compulsory science exams: Physics, Chemistry, Biology and Math. Because of our limited science instruction, we were effectively sitting examinations without the benefit of rigorous instruction, causing consternation among students.

On many evenings I'd curl up against the livestock I'd herded that day, and watch the sky grow dark to reveal sparkling stars, sometimes twinkling and sometimes steady like a distant lamp. When the idea of secondary school turned into reality, I promised myself that I'd study astronomy, learning as much as I could about the lights in the sky, the whys and hows of their movement. I was going to study physics. With no serious science education, my dream would be lost.

Our headmaster sensed the growing discontent among the students and set up a physics experiment for our class. But because his specialization was in Math and not in Physics, the experiment backfired spectacularly, and for students like me who'd clamoured for more instruction in the sciences, this was the last straw. It stretched our patience thin, and we wanted our voices heard, and our concerns taken seriously.

Our strike was careful to exclude the senior four students who were about to write the Ordinary Level Cambridge Certificate examinations, but otherwise it brought the school to its knees, paralyzing all activities.

On the first day, the headmaster and school board tried to reason with us, but negotiations swiftly fell apart, and he sent word to the District Education Office, and to the Ministry of Education. Someone from the District Education office arrived on the second day to negotiate or reason with us, but his efforts failed as well. On the third day, the Minister of Education arrived all the way from Kampala, called an assembly and gave the entire school a dressing down for starting the strike. After the assembly he closed the school and we were told to leave the school immediately.

They sent us to our dormitories, told us to pack our belongings, and board the school lorry which was at the gate ready to take us to town. In the haste of my packing, I took the school radio with me, which I safeguarded as the student entertainment minister.

A few months after everything cooled down, the school reopened, and they invited most of the students back. An investigation into the strike revealed I was one of the ringleaders of the strike. Along with a strong suspicion that I had been smuggling alcohol into the school, they did not invite me back to the school when it reopened. That was a crushing blow, watching my dreams wither before me, and was disappointment far greater than I'd experienced so far.

It is interesting to note that after this strike, the school received new science teachers. Up to this point, no scientists, engineers, mathematicians, or medical professionals had come from Butobere. Even though I lost my place at Siniya, I comfort myself by thinking that without the strike, the science education at the school would have continued to suffer.

After I was dis-invited from Kigezi College Butobere, I needed a plan to salvage my education. I found a private school in Buganda, the central region of Uganda, where I'd sit and hopefully pass my Ordinary Level exams. My father agreed, and because of the time limit we left quickly to find a school.

This wasn't my first trip to Buganda. In 1959 I'd briefly enrolled in Brethren Memorial College Kilyagonja, a junior secondary school near Matuga on Bombo Road. I'd failed to qualify for a place in one of the junior secondary schools near home in Kigezi.

That initial visit was quite a culture shock. I had never ridden in a bus for more than an hour. To get to Brethren Memorial College, we had to board a bus that started its route at six o'clock in the morning, finally arriving in Kampala at six in the evening. The bus ride was an education in the landscape of Uganda. From the steep cold of Kigezi's elevation, we crossed the rolling hills and plateaus of Ankole, and deposited in the sweltering heat much closer to the equator in Buganda.

My brother, Katungi, had been to Kampala before me and was my guide through the evening chaos of the city. I had never seen so many concrete buildings huddled together like chicks afraid to stray far from their mother, and serving no purpose other than house people for work. Vehicles roared past on paved roads that reflected the heat of the day back onto us. The sights and the sounds were overwhelming, but before I acclimated to my new surroundings, we boarded a different bus, the Matuga-Bombo bus, and went to the village where we'd spend the night. My father had arranged accommodation with the founder and owner of the junior school I was going to attend.

I had incredible culture shock the first time I went to Buganda. The language was different, the pace of life was different, the climate was hotter, and the food was different. Even the fruit was different. Having grown up at altitude and among people that raised livestock more than they farmed, I had never eaten mangoes. One day on the way back home from school I was walking behind some children from a neighbouring primary school, and we came across a mango tree and they started throwing stones at the tree to dislodge the fruit. Being an expert marksman, having co-invented a game of throwing stones at moving birds, this was pretty easy. I took aim, threw a stone at a mango, hit it, and it fell to the ground. I did not know whether the mango I had extricated from the tree was somebody else's property, so I quickly tucked it into one of my pockets and ran away to taste this fruit I had never tried before.

When I got home, I found a private spot and sank my teeth into the mango. My taste buds puckered in consternation as my mouth filled with the most sour taste I had ever encountered. I could barely chew it. My mouth flooded with saliva, lips crumpling up, and my eyes watered. I spat the nasty pieces onto the ground and threw the rest of the fruit away, disgusted. The tree did not belong to anybody, but at the time I did not know it, and I became furious at myself for stealing fruit whose taste was so offensive. I did not know that I bit into a raw mango. It was many years before anyone convinced me to eat a mango again.

In my first year in Buganda, I contracted malaria for the very first time and it ravaged my body. My father and mother saw how difficult the first year was, and being so far from home and everything that brought me comfort, and got me a place at Kinyasano Junior Secondary School, now known as Makobore High School near Rukungiri town in Kigezi. I flourished there, passing my exams with grades high enough to get me into Siniya.

With this challenging backdrop from my first experience in Buganda, I returned in 1963 with determination to find a place that offered familiarity, to ease my transition. Even with the expulsion from Siniya, I hadn't hit rock bottom. I chose a place where I was just another anonymous person, with easy access to alcohol. Stuck in my alcoholism and still quite prideful, I didn't think drinking would affect my academics that much. I lived in Bunamwaya, just outside Kampala.

Zana, the bus and taxi stop in Bunamwaya has an interesting history. A well-known and popular lady called Zana owned a famous nightclub near the bus stop. People adopted her name as the shorthand to describe where they were going for the evening. To this day, the trading centre that rose around the bus/taxi stop is still called Zana.

There was no shortage of alcohol, but it differed from the sorghum-based drink I had grown up with. It is a drink distilled from a particular banana plant called waragi, and much more potent than the alcohol I had grown up with. It caused blindness and, in many rumored cases, death. Both central governments, the Ugandan and Buganda governments, outlawed its production, but it did not stop in places like Zana where customers, like myself, were in plenty. Production is cheap, making it the poor man's gin, something I could afford.

A private school called Fellowship High School Nyanama accepted me, and paid the fees to enroll for Senior Four. However, like many private schools there was little-to-no regulation making the quality of education sub par. They were more interested in collecting the fees than educating young people, making the education abysmal. With little authority at the school to enforce discipline, combined with alcohol abuse and poor education, I received a substandard education experience at Fellowship High School.

At the end of Senior Four, all students across Uganda sit a series of national examinations. The British administered them and were The Cambridge Ordinary Level Examination. To qualify to sit the examinations, all students that attended private schools had to pass an English test, known among the students as "The Pink Paper" because they always printed it on pink paper. It should come as no surprise that I did not pass The Pink Paper because I was spectacularly unprepared. I was not allowed to sit for the Cambridge examinations, ending my formal education for many years to come.

After flunking out of school, I was surprisingly upbeat. I felt like I had caught a break and it was finally time to live life on my own terms. Truthfully, I was too proud to return home with the albatross of failure hanging so heavily from my neck. So instead of returning home, I left Zana and moved to the slums in Mulago, in Kampala. The largest government hospital in Uganda, and its adjoining medical school, is on Mulago hill just above the slums. Many Bakiga from

Kigezi, who worked in the mental hospital, or at Makerere University as cooks or casual labourers, lived there.

I found accommodation in a poorly constructed house with tight, small rooms, and made friends with other young and unemployed men like myself. Being around this many young people from home gave me a sense of community. In addition, some Bakiga in the slums brewed omuramba, and the surface familiarity conspired to keep me there for a few months. When we could not afford to buy food, we waited till the evening and raided the mental hospital for scraps of food left over by the patients. On other occasions we crossed the valley and went to Makerere to visit the university students, some of whom I'd known back in school. We would have a meal in their halls of residence and then I would return to the slums in Mulago.

My time in the slums lasted little longer than a few months because the Bakiga I was living with eventually kicked me out. Even though we were from the same part of the country, I did not have any genuine connection to them, and more to that, I was unemployed and addicted to alcohol. Compounded together, they didn't make for an endearing personality or welcome house guest, and I was a strain on their limited resources. I moved out of the slums and looked for a new place to stay. The only place I could think of going was the bus terminal in the centre of Kampala city, run by Uganda Transport Company (UTC). It was a busy terminal where people from all over Uganda, Kenya and Rwanda constantly arrived or left, so a young man seated next to his mattress and wooden box does not draw much attention. Everybody assumed I was probably arriving, leaving, or transferring to another bus.

When I got hungry, I left the bus station and wandered through the city, rummaging through garbage bins for morsels of food. Sometimes

I would venture to Katanga, a slum in the valley between Makerere and Mulago, and if I was lucky, I could run into people I knew, either from Makerere University or the Mulago slums. After a while I finally got homesick, and longed for the familiarity of my language, and the less stressful, slower-paced life of a smaller town. I longed for more than the rotting scraps of discarded food I ate out of the bins, and a bed that was not on the verandah of the UTC central bus terminal. Like the proverbial prodigal son, I just wanted to go back home. But unlike him, I had not yet hit rock bottom. I was still too proud to admit defeat.

In the 1960s a bus ticket from Kampala to Kabale cost 35 shillings, or the equivalent of $7 US at the prevailing exchange rate. In addition, I needed an extra 2 shillings and 10 cents for the bus from Kabale to take me close enough to walk up the steep hill to our home in Karujanga. Having lived on the streets for some time now, I had no money to pay for the ticket.

The days at the bus station turned into months. I became increasingly desperate. I had moved to the bus station thinking I might find work there, but nothing materialized. I dreaded every passing day, consumed with the thought that I would never find the money to go home. I begged and pled with the bus conductors who handled the routes to Kabale to let me travel for free. I learned the name of one of the bus conductors, Mr Lukwago, and pleaded with him every time I saw him, begging him to let me onto the night bus he managed. It took several months to wear him down, and he relented. His one condition was that if the ticket inspector found me, they would leave me behind. Even knowing how risky it was to be abandoned on the side of the highway, I was so destitute; I agreed to his terms and made it all the way to Mbarara without being discovered.

The buses bound for Kabale stopped at a bus station in Mbarara town to refuel, offload passengers, and take on new passengers. Everybody exited the bus and had to reenter the bus after this stop. Unfortunately, there was a UTC ticket inspector in Mbarara checking for tickets, and since I didn't have one, they ordered me off the bus with my luggage 142 kilometres away from Kabale.

Just like Kampala, I ended up staying in the bus terminal in Mbarara for three months, sorting through another set of garbage bins, and trying to convince the bus conductors to let me onto a bus headed to Kabale. The three months I spent in the terminal in Mbarara were agonizing. I was much closer to home, but it was too far to walk, and as the sky darkened every evening, the night fell like the clanging of doors to a prison I could not escape.

One day I got lucky again. A bus conductor took pity on me. He must have seen me more than once, asking to get onto one of the buses. He gave me the same instructions as Mr Lukwago had, promising to leave me by the side of the road if they found me out, but this time I made it all the way to Kabale. The day I arrived in Kabale was truly the end of my exile and my spirit soared like a bird let out of its cage. This was a town I knew, filled with people I knew. Hoards of relatives walked on every street, perched behind shop fronts, conducting all manner of businesses. It felt like a new lease on life.

The sun rose, the famous Kabale fog faded, revealing the landscape I knew and loved. I gave my luggage to a UTC security man promising to return and pay him back, went straight to a familiar drinking joint in the town, never looked back, and never saw my trusted suitcase and mattress again.

As I gazed up at Buhuru bar's sign, a sense of relief washed over my entire body, the familiar tingle of anticipation running up and down my spine. "Kurikayo," someone called, welcoming me home. "Orarugahe?" Another person beckoned "Ija tunywe," inviting me to drink and prompting a fantastic fabrication of my adventures in Buganda, as I downed a well deserved and free mug of muramba.

And just like that, the next chapter of my life began.

Circa 1967, Bishop Tucker School of Divinity, Kampala.

4

Unlikely Redemption

By the evening of my first day back in Kabale, I was completely intoxicated and needed to wash the stench of travel off my body and a semi-comfortable bed to sleep. Two factors influenced my decision. First, there needed to be some family connection, and second, it had to be close to an omuramba brewery. I ended up in Ruhita sub-zone, Rwakaraba, where my grandmother's relatives lived, and where most of the omuramba brewed in Kabale came from. Bugongi and Kigongi hosted the other two big breweries, but Rwakaraba was omuramba central.

A few weeks after I settled in Rwakaraba, I joined a gang of boys who were also unemployed alcoholics, and we appointed ourselves brewery inspectors and taste testers. The scam we came up with allowed us to bar hop, moving from one brewery to another, claiming we were sent by the bars that wanted to buy their omuramba. Sellers who brewed in their homes, desperate to make a sale, invited us in, and handed us long straws to drain the liquid out of the dregs (omurituro) at the bottom of the brew.

During these drinking sprees, I wondered what happened in the lives of the people I had gone to school with, curious to find out what they had done with their lives and how far their education took them. This curiosity took me on walks from Rwakaraba to the centre of Kabale town (about 2 kilometres) to a place they liked to gather called "Kisementi" where they gathered. The bar leaned against a concrete retainer wall built to prevent mudslides from blocking Kabale's main street. It was near the bus terminal and the post office where many of the young people I knew gathered to buy the daily newspaper, Uganda Argus, catch up on the news, and share stories about our contemporaries. I listened for tidbits about the schools they attended and about new events happening in their lives. When they dispersed to go home, I walked back to Rwakaraba, head filled with envy and shattered dreams, and cocooned myself in my strange, aimless life.

It must have been at one of those meetings in Kisementi that I learned about a private Junior Secondary school in Buyanja, which needed to fill a few teaching positions. They wanted to recruit young men and women who had completed Senior Four, assuming it was sufficient qualification to teach at the school. Armed with this information, I travelled to Buyanja and landed a job teaching English and Religious Education.

After my time in Rwakaraba, this job gave me a semblance of normalcy. I had a regular job and drew a monthly salary of 120 shillings. With it, I got accommodation in the local trading centre, and being an alcoholic, the rest of my pay fuelled my drinking habit.

The headmaster and several teachers on staff loved to drink as much as I did and became my regular drinking buddies. The headmaster preferred waragi, while the rest of us, who did not have as much money, settled for a banana-based potent called oruhuro.

We started drinking as soon as school was out, and by the end of the evening, we were a stumbling mess of loud men, causing chaos in the streets. We were not very good educators, severely unqualified for the job of educating children, more concerned with making enough money to service our addictions.

During this time I reestablished contact with Topher. Our letters to each other had stopped when I was homeless in Kampala, but we reconnected when she went to Nyakasura School for her senior secondary education. The administration at her new school allowed their students to receive letters, making our lines of communication a little easier. Through our letters, sporadic meetings, and conversations, I became very fond of her and hoped that one day I would marry her if she was willing. On several occasions, I'd told her how proud I would be if she became the mother of my children, which made me feel suave. I thought it was the kind of thing women wanted to hear.

One day I received a letter from her saying she was no longer interested in continuing our correspondence or our relationship. I was devastated and went straight to the bar where I bought a bottle of gin. I put it to my lips and drank as hard and fast as I could without breathing, hoping the shock to my system would knock me out. Maybe if I was inebriated enough, I would feel relief from the all-consuming pain that twisted in my heart. Laying alone in my bed that night, sleep evaded me. Topher's rejection loomed over me, a dark suffocating cloud that broke my heart again and again. I wondered if she broke up with me because she heard about my burgeoning alcoholism, but it was too late. The girl of my dreams had dumped me and I was heartbroken.

From this point on, I had an excuse to descend to the depth of my addiction, and things went from bad to worse. One evening in the routine of getting severely inebriated, I got into an argument with the proprietor of the establishment we were hanging out at, and I insulted him. He shoved me to the floor; I landed with a thud on the grimy floor right in front of my colleagues and other evening revelers. Before my shaking legs could raise me up from it, he kicked me right in the face. I woke up the next morning with a bruised and swollen face, and rushed to the nearest medical centre, fearing that I had a cracked skull. After a few tests, I was told that my skull was intact, and that there was no head trauma save for a wounded face muscle, so I returned home. A letter from the owner of the school was waiting for me when I got home, informing me they had fired me. Without a job, and without money, it was not long before I was back to homelessness on the streets of Rukungiri town.

I bounced around for a while, first ending up in Bugangari, 16 kilometres outside Rukungiri, and then further north to Bwambara, 33 kilometres away from Rukungiri. At the time my elder brother, Ndyomugenyi lived in Bwambara. I went to him to try my hand at agriculture. The cash crop farmers were going crazy over was tobacco, and I figured that together, we could use his land and make money from the harvest. I sold the idea to him and he enthusiastically said yes.

Unfortunately, my brother was as much of an alcoholic as I was. Our lofty plans to grow tobacco crumbled and fell by the wayside. Tobacco is a labour-intensive crop, and we were too busy trying to find our next drink to prepare the ground, plant the crops, or do any meaningful, intensive agricultural work. In the end, nothing materialized from our plans to make a living through agriculture, and defeated, I left Bwambara.

One of our drinking buddies told me I could walk from Bwambara to Kabale on a special route. The shortest one was a 100 kilometer hike from Bwambara, through Nyamirama and Kambuga, all the way to Kabale. I set off and walked and hitch-hiked all the way back to Kabale, where I returned to my old stomping grounds in Rwakaraba. There was solace in being in a place that was so familiar.

Rwakaraba was just as I left it; the hideout for unemployed youth. Young men still ran scams through local bars pretending to be "brew inspectors". There were still young women who served as bartenders who we hit on every chance we got. I took up as an entertainer in the bars I visited, playing drums on a contraption made by stretching cowhide over the mouth of an old petroleum barrel. These were drums normally used to call people to worship on Sunday mornings, but now served as our musical instruments, helping us provide entertainment on our nightly benders. I led the singing, pulling my repertoire from songs I remembered hearing years back on the stolen radio from Siniya. When I ran out of those, I led them in church hymns, and we sang with great gusto, shouting at the top of our inebriated lungs.

With no employment, I became an entrepreneur entertainer and was paid for my services with drinks. At the end of the night when everybody left, I slept on a bench in the bar I had performed at. Then the almighty jukebox was introduced, and radically changed entertainments. For fifty cents, you played back one song of your choosing, and for a whole shilling you got three complete songs. My job as an entertainer became obsolete, and my steady supply of drinks dwindled.

I was destitute once again, without a roof over my head or pillow to sleep on. The clothes I left Bwambara with became threadbare, falling off my emaciated frame because I wore them every day without washing them. The only saving grace I had was my overcoat, which we called a Kabuti. It served a dual purpose, a cover for my near nakedness during the day, and a blanket at night. After all this time, it was the only possession I had left.

The servers kicked me out of the bars in the morning when they returned to prepare for early customers. I grew accustomed to rousing from the stupor of drunken sleep, and thrown out every morning, along with the rubbish from the bars onto the streets of Rwakaraba.

Breakfast as we know it now, with tea and bread, was not a thing. Instead, the morning meal of choice was a sorghum-based drink called obushera. Incidentally, omuramba is made by first creating obushera and then fermenting it. For alcoholics like myself, obushera was not quite enough as breakfast. We wanted the real thing, omuramba.

In the mornings government workers stopped by the bars for breakfast. They had to arrive at work sober, and didn't finish the entire cup of omuramba with their breakfast. The homeless drunks dove after the leftovers, draining every drop for their breakfast, trembling with pleasure as our alcohol-addled minds were satisfied. I was among them, tipping the remaining dregs into my empty belly, hoping they'd fill me up till the evening drinking started.

One morning that seemed like every other, I started the day getting kicked out of a bar and hunting for the scraps left by government workers. I stumbled out of one bar and started my daily walk to the city centre. As I remember it, the streets of Kabale were eerily empty. No cars belched lung-clogging black plumes, no bicycles laden with the day's harvest crawled past, no people occupied with dreams of the future or worries of the past, dodging the reek emanating off my body. It seemed like the whole world emptied and I was alone walking that section of the Kabale-Kisoro road.

In the middle of the road stood a mirror reflection of myself, laid bare for all eyes to see, including everything my kabuti hid. The rancid fumes coming off my body burned my nostrils. I saw lice crawling from my matted hair, and walking freely on well-worn highways on my kabuti. Ticks embedded in the creases of my arms and legs pulsed as they sucked the life out of me, partially hidden by the hairiness of my body. My feet throbbed, and looking at them saw they were cracked and swollen, oozing yellow pus, attracting flies and other biting insects. I'd later find out that I was in the advanced stages of kwashiorkor, having lived on omuramba and nothing else for almost a year.

Something deeper happened at that moment. While I saw my physical self and experienced revulsion for it, like x-ray or CT scans reveal what's underneath skin and sinew, I saw deeper, more exhaustive information. Right before my horrified eyes, I saw my internal organs turn from healthy pink flesh, withering in some areas, and exploding with pus and maggots in others, turning the dull grey-brown of death.

A voice spoke to me in clear English, thrusting me from the waking nightmare into the bright light of day. "Do you want to live, or do you want to die?"

An ache rose out of the depth of my soul, a wrenching cry that spread through my core, reaching for the life draining from my body, and burst in a shout that echoed all around me, "I want to live!"

I do not know how long this experience was. It could have been a couple of seconds, or minutes, or even hours, but I had chosen life. It was the transformative, out-of-body experience that became the staff I leaned on as I crawled out of the debauchery that led to gaping jaws of death, compelling me to change direction.

That day, I decided to return home. The very first step back to life.

My parents lived 28 kilometres from Kabale town, and having just realized the true shape my feet were in, I knew I could not walk that far. They were too sick and inflamed to carry me home. Having lived as a beggar on the streets of Kabale, asking for money to drink or picking up discarded cigarette butts for a quick smoke, I was used to harassing strangers for help. After my out-of-body experience, things were different. I went into the town and begged for 2 shillings and 10 cents, the exact amount for a bus ride from Kabale to the bus station at Nyinamuronzi, which was as close to my parents' home as I could get.

Lots of people turned me down because I was a known beggar they'd give money to, and had seen me a few hours earlier stumbling around drunk. One kind person gave me the bus fare, and to this day I know they were an angel sent by God, because I cannot recall seeing their face before. I went straight to the bus station and bought a ticket for the evening bus to make sure I didn't spend the money on cigarettes, once again trapping myself in Kabale.

For the first time in a year, I was ashamed of the way I looked. I did not want to show up at home in broad daylight in case people saw the mess I was in. In addition, my father was a person of high standing in the village, and I did not want to shame him with my arrival. I thought it better for him if I arrived at home at night; the darkness masking my state.

On Friday evening I took the bus to Nyinamuronzi, and walked the final 3 kilometer stretch home to Karujanga. I remember it like it was yesterday. I knocked on my mother's door, battling anxiety and shame, and she opened it, not knowing who was outside. A kerosene lamp in her hands illuminated her face, and as soon as she recognized me, she broke down and wept. After a few moments, she gathered herself, put her arms around me, hugged me like only moms can, and greeted me the way Bakiga do when they haven't seen each other in a long time.

The last time my mother saw me, I left home for a school in Buganda. I had packed all my belongings in a wooden box, rolled up my mattress, and left. Here I was, returning to her with nothing. My body was broken, wracked with disease, pain throbbing everywhere I touched. I was an alcohol addict, stripped of my belongings, and my lofty dreams. My physical state,, crushed as I was, couldn't hide the change in my soul. A miracle had happened. From the day I chose life, I lost my appetite for alcohol. The hold addiction had over my life was broken. I was never the same again.

My mother drew me into the house, and gave me the first meal I had eaten in months, then led me to my old bed, a wood frame with rope strung across to support a mat or a mattress. She spread a mat over the ropes and I lay down to sleep. This should have been uncomfortable, but was the first time in over a year that I had slept on anything other than a bare floor or a bench in a bar. I fell asleep, comfortable, sober, and slept like a baby.

The next day the air smelled fresh. First order of business was a long-overdue shower, and washing the lice and dirt out of my kabuti. My mother gave me one of her cloth wraps to cover me while I waited for my coat to dry.

In my drunken haze I lived day to day caring little what day of the week it was. The day I washed my clothes and was sober was Saturday.

The following day I was eager to attend a church service, so I kept a keen eye on my kabuti to make sure it was dry enough to hide my nakedness.

Sunday came, and I went to church. With no clothes under my kabuti, I chose to arrive late to make sure I sat at the back of the church. There were no benches arranged in neat pews, so we all sat on the floor. Knowing that in Anglican Churches the liturgy involves a lot of sitting and standing, I did not want to put anybody sitting behind me in a difficult situation should they see my bare bottom.

When I got to the church, it was as full as I had remembered. I shuffled to a space in the back and recognized many familiar faces. The call to worship was the same as was the confession my father loved. The opening prayers and the collect were exactly as I remembered. We stood up to sing an old revival hymn, one I'd used as entertainment at the bars in Rwakaraba. It rang with different meaning, striking at chords in my heart that humed with potency and power I'd never felt. Like a drink of cold water on a sweltering day, it refreshed parched land deep down inside my soul. I saw that my years of rebellion, pride, and alcoholism was the search for this very thing thrumming in my chest.

THIS refreshing.

THIS relationship.

THIS love.

THIS grace.

THIS mercy.

THIS power.

The omushomesa stood to speak after the hymn, but I could not pay attention to what he said. I was captive to the words of the hymn we sang, and the wind of revival in that small, rural church. After his message, we stood to sing another hymn that spoke directly to my journey to this point. It is about a person who had been in rebellion, but when he heard the gospel of Jesus Christ, was convicted, repented of their sins and was saved. Having returned home only two nights prior, after years of separation, pride, and desolation, I knew that the song was about me. A new journey was about to start in my life. One chapter closed and a new one began. I spent years at death's door, every night of blackout drunkenness like a suicide attempt, and God was about to take my life and write a new story for it.

As Christ's followers, we say that the day you put your faith and trust in Him is a rebirth. In Uganda, we refer to you as being "Born Again". On that first morning in church, I was reborn. The old me was laid to rest, and I was given the gift of a new beginning.

In the second chapter of the letter to the church in Galatia, the apostle Paul writes this:

The life I live in the body, I live by faith in the Son of God who loved me and gave himself for me.

- Galatians 2:20

I did not give my life to Christ that morning, but He took hold of me and I knew I wanted more of what I'd found that Sunday morning.

The week following that service, my mother sent me to a tailor to have new clothes made. I got a pair of trousers, and she gave me a little extra to buy a shirt so that I would not have to wear my old trusty kabuti anymore. A symbolic rebirth, just like the one I experienced at church, and the feeling of cleansing I had received at church, I was reborn into my family. I was bathed, shaved, fed, and clothed as a son of the home.

Let's sing this song born-again Bakiga love to sing.

Arantangaza Yesu we arantangaza!

Okwiha omuntu omukasasiro,

akamunabisa, akamusiiga, akamujweka,

Yesu we arantangaza!

Jesus amazes me!

Rescues a person from the garbage heap,

Washes, anoints, and dresses them.

Jesus is amazing!

This song is my testimony. A young man rescued from the garbage heap, washed, anointed, and dressed by Jesus.

In the months to come, I received sad news that many of the young men in my former gang died within the first three months after I'd left. It could have been me. My life story could have ended in a back alley behind one of the bars, a severely malnourished young man. I know deep in my heart that I would have been one of them, and understand how blessed I am that God reached down and plucked me out of the mess I had made of my life.

I continued to go to church after this transformative first weekend back home and joined the youth group. After a little while, I yearned to return to education, and it began a whole new chapter of my life.

5

Unlikely Reset

For many years the Ugandan education system was designed so that most students who started in primary one would eventually fail. The higher you went in your education, the fewer schools there were. There were fewer junior secondary schools than primary schools, fewer secondary schools than junior high, and only a handful of tertiary institutions if you completed Senior Four. If you completed Senior Six, there was only one university in the country with a few spots.

For someone like me, who flunked out of high school before completing Senior Four, the chances of getting back into school were limited. I was in my early twenties in 1966 when I returned home, and not eligible to return to Senior Three. Part of the rehabilitation of my life was education, but with the limited options it would take a miracle to be accepted to any school. Even though I wanted to return to my education as part of that rehabilitation, I knew I had very few options.

My brother-in-law, Reverend Solomon Bekunda proved to be a lifeline. He married my eldest sister Bakataaka (Loi) and witnessed my slow descent to the gaping mouth of the grave when I lived on the streets. Encouraged by the progress I made after my return, and my involvement in church, he advised me to consider becoming an ordained reverend of the Anglican church.

The thought had never crossed my mind, nor had I thought it a viable option. Most experiences with ordained ministers were negative. I'd received judgement and condemnation from them, as a young boy in church school, all the way through high school, and eventual years on the street. I despised the profession and except for my brother-in-law, did not like being around them.

An ultra-conservative group, a remnant of the East African Revival, had a powerful influence over the church. These "balokole" were an equally intimidating and judgmental group, and any move towards ordination would put me squarely in their sights.

While I wasn't drinking alcohol anymore, I still smoked cigarettes. Church leaders already suspicious of my rapid change from alcoholism to sobriety could use this habit against me. All they knew was the young man who squandered years of his life consumed by alcohol and deliberate homelessness. My acceptance into ordination would be a hurdle, filled with obstacles too many to count. Sensing my resistance to his advice, Solomon stayed persistent, eager in his desire to see me take some direction as I gained a hold of my life. It took a lot of thought and meaningful conversations with both Loi and Solomon, but I relented, deciding it could be worth a try.

When I started my journey to ordination, candidates went through several layers of approval and recommendation. The first hurdle was getting approval and a recommendation from the leadership at the church you attended. The recommendation got passed to the parish level, and if they determined eligibility, they sent a recommendation to the regional diocese, where the diocesesan staff made the final recommendation to the Bishop.

Having avoided church up to this point, I did not know any of these steps and ended up circumventing the entire process. I wrote an application letter directly to the Bishop of Kigezi and to everybody's surprise, mine included, they invited me to the interview.

The day of the interview rolled around, and I donned my freshly washed trousers and white shirt, and travelled early to Rugarama. The enormous cathedral and diocesan offices were on Rugarama hill, a place where Siniya boys attended church services. On the way to the interview, I bought a cigarette, intending to smoke it on the way home after the interview. The cigarette I bought was the last one in the packet, and the shopkeeper gave the entire empty packet to me, and I tucked it in my front shirt pocket.

An Englishman called Richard Lyth chaired the panel that interviewed me. He was the former rector at Rugarama Cathedral when I attended Siniya. I do not remember most of the interview. I was very nervous, and in typical fashion, had not prepared well enough for the interview. When they asked why I wanted to start the path to ordination, I blurted out Isaiah 6:8.

Then I heard the voice of the Lord saying, "Whom shall I send?
And who will go for us?"
And I said, "Here am I. Send me!"

Isaiah 6:8

Even now, I cannot say where the answer came from, but it didn't matter because I didn't pass the interview. As I left Rugarama, walking down the steep hill back to Kabale town reflecting on the questions asked and the answers I'd provided, I had an overwhelming desire to smoke, a crutch I used to decompress and de-stress. As I pulled out the almost-empty cigarette packet from my front pocket, it hit me. The cigarette packet must have shown through my shirt. Clearly this contributed to the decision to decline my application for ordination.

This rejection did not deter me. At the core of my being, I was convinced this was the next path my life should take. I reapplied for ordination, finding myself in front of the Bishop and his panel one year later, better prepared and cigarette packets absent. I passed the interview and received sponsorship for theological training and eventual ordination.

In 1967 I travelled to Bishop Tucker Theological College in Mukono, assigned a room in Mackay House, and as I looked around my room, hands caressing the blanket that covered my bed, I marvelled at being back in the education system. My life had taken a terrible detour for a few years. God rescued me and put me on a path that I hadn't considered for myself.

When I arrived, all I had was a wooden box containing a few sparse belongings and a blanket for my bed. The school's instructions said I needed to bring my own bedsheets, but we could not afford them in addition to the cost of getting me to Mukono. Even without them, or belongings to decorate my room, joy overwhelmed me, and I was unbelievably happy and excited about the next phase.

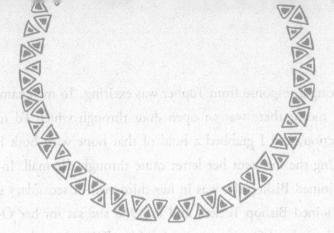

6

Unlikely Love

That first night, I was desperate to share my joy with someone, specifically Topher Tumwijuke, but I was not sure if she wanted to talk to me after our last correspondence. Even though she ended our relationship a few years earlier, I had not stopped thinking about her. I tried to do the manly thing and forget about her, but all efforts failed.

I took a chance, pulled out a piece of paper from the notebook the registration desk gave me, and wrote her a letter. She was at Nyakasura School in Fort Portal. I figured that since I was back to sanity, she would be more receptive to communication. I told her all about the events that transpired in my life since we last wrote to each other, and about my admission to Bishop Tucker College. A week later, I received a response from her saying she was thrilled for me and glad that I had turned my life around.

Getting a response from Topher was exciting. To my enamoured mind it meant there was an open door through which I'd reclaim her affection, and I grabbed a hold of that hope with both hands, responding the moment her letter came through the mail. In 1967 when I joined Bishop she was in her third year of secondary school when I joined Bishop Tucker, and in 1968 she sat for her O-Level Cambridge School Certificate examinations. Being the polar opposite of me at that age, she was a studious pupil, coming at the top of her class and completing her O-Levels.

In one of her letters she told me after she finished her O-Level exams, she had plans to visit her brother Stephen in Kampala. Mukono is a mere 22 kilometers from Kampala, and with a little detective work, I figured out where Stephen lived. When she came to Kampala, I visited them both, an incredible reunion. Stephen, her brother and my friend from Siniya, did not disapprove of my interest in his sister, making my meetings with Topher much easier.

When I visited, we went for long walks through parks and Kampala's streets, talking and laughing about anything and everything. One important conversation revolved around her education plans. As a subsistence farmer, her father could not afford the school fees for A-Level education, having to support eight other children besides her and Stephen.

She seriously considered joining the teacher's training college at Kyambogo, where she could fulfil her desire to become a secondary school teacher and be close to Bishop Tucker in Mukono. One day as she accompanied me to the bus stop on my way back to College, we had a chance meeting with some of her former schoolmates in a similar situation. They were coming from the Veterinary Training Institute in Entebbe and found out that there were vacancies for people who wished to make the switch to veterinary sciences.

In the days that followed, I waited to receive communication about her admission to the teacher training college in Kyambogo, not thinking she had given serious thought to the veterinary option, but it turns out that she had. To my surprise, she wrote to let me know she changed her mind and enrolled in a veterinary medicine diploma program at the institute in Entebbe.

Mukono is east of Kampala, and Entebbe is south west. With the transportation options of the time, getting to Entebbe required better planning, but was definitely easier than travelling to Kambuga. To get to Entebbe, I rode a bus from Mukono to the bus station in Kampala, and then a second one from Kampala to Entebbe.

The veterinary institute is outside Entebbe, and further along the peninsula, close to the airport. Being my first trip there I didn't realize just how far away it was. I had to take the bus, walk from the bus station past the houses at the end of the town, then walk all the way around the airport to the east along the shores of lake Victoria. As I walked along the road near the lake I noticed dark, heavy rain clouds over the lake racing across the sky, but I persisted thinking that I could make it to the institute before it got to land.

Storms that form over the lake near Entebbe fly towards the land faster than the ones I was familiar with, and without quick access to a building for shelter, and I got drenched from head to toe in this typical tropical soaker. It hit hard and fast, dissipating as quickly as it came. In a few minutes the sun was out again, and there I was on the road to meet the object of my love, clothes sticking to my body, dripping into my sloshing, waterlogged shoes. It looked like someone had rescued me from drowning in the lake. A terrible look for a suiter. I could not appear at her door looking like that. It would not make a good impression. Luckily, a boy from my village attended the vet institute, and I hunted him down to dry out in his room. When my clothes and shoes were partially dry and I was presentable, I went to Topher's dorm and asked for her. My visit was shorter than I had planned, and before long I was back on the road racing to catch all the buses back to Mukono.

Having reestablished contact with Topher, I determined I would not mess things up a second time. I did whatever it took to make the journey to Entebbe to visit her. When I visited, I left early in the morning so we could spend as much of the day together, and then returned to Mukono in time to get my studying done. When I could not visit, I telephoned. There was only one phone at Bishop Tucker, and it was in the Principal's house. Amos Betungura needed convincing in order to let me make occasional calls to Topher from his house, but allowed it. The vet institute in Entebbe had a public phone booth that students used, and Topher took my calls at pre-arranged times.

One dull afternoon, one of my schoolmates approached me to say I had a visitor. It was unusual for me to receive visitors at Mukono, so I rushed to my room to see who it was. There she was. Topher hailed from a conservative background, making it improper for her to visit a man on her own. She loaded her sister and brother, Karen and David, into a bus and brought them with her so we could see each other. I didn't know what to do with impromptu visitors because I never had any. Sophisticated friends rescued me, scouring the campus for drinks, and sitting with us to make small talk. Refreshed, I took Topher and her siblings on a tour of the college campus.

As with any small college, word got around that Mugarura had a girlfriend, and was brazenly parading her around the campus. Fashion-forward Topher was dressed in a miniskirt, a downright scandal at the theology college. Her exposed legs desecrated the holy place, and she was here to see a man. The judgement of the religious leaders, the very thing that kept me away from the church, reared its ugly head. A requirement of study at the theological college was to abstain from cross-gender relationships, and here I was breaking the rules in public with a pretty young lady in a miniskirt.

Thankfully, I had wholehearted support from my friends at college. They got to know her, loved how smart she was, and how passionate about her views of the World and the decisions she made for her future. They approved of my desire to marry her.

In 1969, my father was walking home when a cyclist struck him from behind, hurtling him to the ground. He brushed himself off, got back up, and resumed his trek. By the time he got home, he was in a lot of pain, but went to sleep hoping that rest would return him to health. His condition didn't improve after a few days, and my family took him to Kabale hospital where they admitted him. By that time, the internal injuries from the accident had progressed too far for the medical professionals to help, and in a few days he was dead.

This unexpected news hit me hard. We developed a close relationship after I returned from my self-imposed exile, strengthening even after I left for Bishop Tucker. Having been a church teacher himself, he was eager to engage me in theological debate, challenge the holes in my scant understanding of the Bible, and share his wisdom about church leadership. On my visits home, we had long conversations about the church and the Bible.

In particular, I remember him questioning me about the apostle Paul, and about his conversion journey. He challenged me about the early church and the life of Saul, asking where the seed of conversion was planted.

I knew about Saul's supernatural encounter in Acts 9, but this was not the answer my father was looking for. He told me about an event earlier in Saul's life, which turned out to be the seed of his eventual conversion. In Acts 7, Saul witnessed Stephen's stoning, one of the early leaders of the church. He contended that Saul's presence at the stoning was when the seed of faith was planted, and the moment Jesus entered his heart. You could draw a straight line from that moment to Saul's conversion, church planting and eventual martyrdom in Rome.

I loved my conversations with my father, and both he and I looked forward with great anticipation to my eventual graduation from seminary. I knew how much my journey into ministry meant to him, and when he died before I graduated, I was devastated.

At the time Bishop Tucker offered two tiers of diplomas. A three-year certificate that people with a similar education level as mine could achieve, after which you were eligible to sit an exam to qualify for another three-year diploma awarded by Makerere University. I finished the first tier diploma in 1969 at the same time that Topher started her second year of veterinary college. Graduates from seminary usually returned to their sending diocese and upon ordination were assigned a parish. Just like other graduates from Kigezi, I planned to return to Kabale and go through the ordination process.

I decided to ask Topher for her hand in marriage. Even though we had been seeing each other for a while, she did not immediately accept my proposal. Her father was a lay church leader, and she had a frontline seat to the hostility and politics that exist in church leadership. She wanted no part of it. Even though she liked me, she was not sure she wanted to spend the rest of her life married to a church worker, and told me she needed time to consider it. Even though I had fallen deeply in love with Topher, I gave her space to make her decision without interference. I wasn't sure she would accept my proposal because the hurt inflicted on her family by the church ran pretty deep.

At the end of my first-tier diploma, I sat the entrance exam into the second-tier diploma program awarded by Makerere, which I passed. I applied for mature-entry to the program and was admitted. Mature-entry to the university is an alternative path to tertiary level education for older students applied through non-traditional A-Level examinations. When I was admitted to the program I was told that, because of my first-tier diploma, I could complete it in two years instead of the required three. And for the two years I was in the second-tier diploma program, it allowed Topher room to weigh her options and see if she wanted to build a future with me.

One of our favourite places to visit during our courtship was Namirembe Cathedral, one of the biggest and oldest Anglican Cathedrals in Uganda. On the wings of the hill, you have spectacular views of Kampala city in all directions. We agreed to meet at Namirembe and spent the entire day fasting, praying, and discussing our future together. Topher came with an exhaustive list of questions. She wanted to make sure there were no skeletons hiding in my closet, and that the person she was considering spending her life with was the genuine article. I answered her questions as best and honestly as I could, and after the interrogation, she finally agreed to marry me.

The girl I had fallen for so many years before agreed to marry me. The woman who had broken up with me because I was leading a self-destructive life saw enough of a change in me, and I could hardly believe it. It was almost too good to be true. I was in heaven.

We immediately started planning our wedding and set a date. 1st January 1972 at St Peter's Cathedral, Rugarama, Kabale.

I was so excited. I had to tell someone. My best friend from college was Reverend Benoni Ogwal. I persuaded Topher to go to his house for a quick visit and when we got there, I excitedly told him the news. He was one person who supported our relationship, and I asked him to be the best man at our wedding, which he agreed to. As we left his home for our respective colleges, we were the happiest couple in the world.

Unsurprisingly, Topher graduated in 1970 at the top of her class. She was always a more focused and disciplined student than I was. She received a first-class diploma in Animal Husbandry specializing in cattle and milk production. Soon after her graduation, she got a job with the Ministry of Agriculture and was posted to Kigezi district headquartered in Kabale. She was the first female veterinary officer with the Ministry of Agriculture in our region and I was incredibly proud of her. It also helped that they posted her close to the headquarters of my sending diocese, and close enough to her parents that she could introduce me, and discuss our upcoming marriage.

Among the Bakiga, it is rude to introduce yourself to your in-laws. Instead, you go through an elaborate series of choreographed meetings. In each one, you do not speak for yourself. You are not old enough, respectable enough, or of equal standing to your bride's father. A person of high standing and good repute in your family, someone her family will respect acts as the spokesperson on your behalf. This person could be your father, an exceedingly rare choice. Most of the time it is an uncle, an older brother, or a community leader from your village.

If you happened to be interested in a Mukiga woman, but you were not from the same tribe, her family would assign a Katerarume, a go-between, to assist with the introduction between the two cultures to avoid any cross-cultural landmines.

My brother-in-law, Reverend Solomon Bekunda, was my spokesperson, and visited Topher's family to formally introduce the matter of our wedding. He was a good representative of our family because he shared my father-in-law's job as a church worker. I was very grateful for Solomon because in the absence of my father; I needed not just a father figure, but somebody to help me keep everything on track. As was the custom of the time, her family asked for a dowry of six cows, and I had five cows to my name. My brother-in-law donated one of his cows to meet the required number, and with that, all they had to do was to agree on the date we had set.

Topher and I chose the first of January 1972, but her father objected. He felt it was too rushed and said we needed more time to prepare, a sentiment that turned out to be prophetic. Eventually he agreed to it, and we confirmed our wedding day.

During this back-and-forth introduction and negotiation with Topher's family, I was in Mukono finishing my studies. The vice chancellor of Makerere, Professor Frank Kalimuzo, presided over our graduation at college, and was anxious to return to Kabale to help with the wedding preparations that had started without me.

When I got home, I found out the dowry delivery date was the Kuhingira on Friday the 31st of December 1971, a day before the wedding. Delivering the cows was more complicated than I thought. The cows were in Karujanga, and in an ideal situation we would have hired a lorry and sent them the day before, but we had no money. Our only option was to walk the cows 108 Km for two days from

Karujanga to Kambuga. I split the journey with my eldest brother, Ndyomugenyi.

Three days before the Kuhingira I got up at 4 AM, opened the creaky gate of the wood pen for the last time. I felt the pang of loss as I let the last of my beloved cows out of the gate. It was an emotional moment. It was the last time we were going to open this pen, and I loved my cows. I was comforted by the thought that this loss would be rewarded by receiving the woman I loved, but it was a bitter-sweet moment.

Our first stop was Kabale to receive the final promised cow from Reverend Bekunda. Two of his sons, my nephews, joined me for the first leg of the journey. On the first day we walked 61 km, stopping to rest at a church at Ahamurwa on the Kabale - Kisoro road. At night we collapsed with exhaustion, and when we woke up, found that the famished cows had been awake for a few hours, helping themselves to the church teacher's garden outside the church.

I immediately went to the church teacher and asked for forgiveness. They do not pay church teachers well in rural parts of Uganda, and to supplement their income, they take care of their families through subsistence farming. The church teacher was very kind and forgave the damage. He prayed with us, fed us, and sent us off on the second day of our walk.

The second leg of the walk took us on a near vertical climb from Ahamurwa to Kerere hill, which in my estimation, is one of the highest hills in Uganda. If Kerere hill were 10 meters higher, they would classify it as a mountain. A chilly breeze swept in from the east that morning, turning both man and beast inwards, each lowering our heads as we climbed the hill. Below us in the valleys a fog covered the landscape, with hills rising out from the fog like islands on a big white lake.

To the west of Kerere hill is an unobstructed view of the Muhavura range, with Muhabura's misty peak towering above the range. The scenery on the climb up Kerere hill is breathtaking, but that morning there wasn't much time to enjoy it. We got close to the top of Kerere hill at a place called Karengere and heard the bus from Kabale labouring up the hill. Ndyomugenyi was on the bus, coming to take over the second part of the journey so I could return to Kabale and prepare for the Kuhingira. When they came up beside us, he disembarked and took over the cows and my nephews for the rest of the journey down Kerere hill, through Kanungu to Kambuga.

Once we made the exchange, I waited in the cold for another bus going the opposite way, coming from Rukungiri and ending in Kabale. After a few cold, groggy hours, the bus chugged up the hill coughing black fumes and I flagged it down. Exhausted from the long, gruelling trek, I jumped off at my brother-in-law's house to pick up the Kuhingirwa program, went to the house Topher had rented in Kabale and fell into a deep dreamless sleep.

The next morning I walked from Topher's home in Bugongi to get a haircut, then walked to Solomon Bekunda's home where we waited for our transportation to Kambuga. My brother, Katungi, who worked in Kampala, had a car and offered it as transportation for the trip. Besides my brother's car, we expected two more cars - one from my cousin, and another from my best man Ben Ogwal. That morning, not a single one of them arrived. Solomon hired a car with three seats to take us to Kambuga and bring us back in the evening. The best price we could negotiate at such short notice was 120 shillings, which was a lot of money; the equivalent of a full month's salary.

I was eager to get to Kambuga to find Ndyomugenyi, my nephews, and the cows. Thankfully, their journey from Karengere was smooth and unmolested. They made it most of the way to a little village called Rugeyo and spent the night at the local church parish with a generous parish priest, Reverend Jack Kabahikyeho. They arrived late at night, way past dinnertime, but this amazing couple took them in, fed them, and then Reverend Jack watched over the cows at night to make sure they did not eat the plants in his sorghum garden. The next morning, they gave them a hearty breakfast and sent them on their way.

For many years now, parish priests of rural communities have served a unique function. They're not just responsible for the spiritual education and literacy of their communities. They open their homes to strangers passing through the parish and need a place to stay for the night. Walking the cows from Karujanga to Kambuga without their help and hospitality would have been impossible. They opened their houses to us, welcomed and fed us, and made sure we knew how to get to the next stop on our journey. I will forever be grateful for parish priests in rural communities.

By the time we got to Kambuga, my brother had arrived close to Topher's family home. I was happy that he made it so the function could continue with no complications. We took a quick minute to get ourselves in order and then started the final walk to the gathering place. When we arrived outside the home, traditional drums echoed through the hillside to signify that the function was about to start.

As is the custom, they choreographed an elaborate custom before the ceremony could begin. Two of Topher's brothers went out to inspect the cows. Among the Bakiga, after they agree to the dowry , two representatives from the woman's family go to the home of the man's family to make sure they are good cows, healthy and well fed. This ceremony is called "Okujugisa". At Okujugisa some families go to their neighbours to borrow cows for the inspection to create the illusion that they are wealthy. Then at the Kuhingira, different cows they deliver the cows.

To guard against the deception, a second ceremony developed called "Okujuga". Before the Kuhingira started, the representatives who visited the man's home at Okujugisa verified that the cows being delivered were the same ones seen on their initial visit. Upon our arrival at Topher's family home, her brothers marched out to "Okujuga" and make sure we were people of our word.

They completed their inspection and were satisfied, the drums sounded a second time and we proceeded into their home. Topher's family home is on the side of a steep hill outside the centre of Kambuga, and her father and mother, Samwiiri and Justine Turahi, had a gigantic party prepared. Dozens gathered to send Topher off, and as we walked down the hill to the house, the guests stood to welcome us, naturally creating a path that led to an open structure, Ekitirirwa, made for the occasion.

Samwiiri Turahi was a devout Christian and nothing, I mean absolutely nothing, started in his home without prayer. A priest came out, started with a prayer, announced an opening hymn, and while we were singing, he went into the house to bring the bride out from her room to the worship service that would precede the Kuhingira.

While we sang the hymn, Topher and her entourage emerged from the house. She was right in the middle of a group of a colourful splash of beautifully adorned young women, sisters and cousins, but I could pick her out of the gaggle immediately. She was draped in a gorgeous Indian Sari we picked out together. It was specially tailored for her by an Indian seamstress in Kampala. She was radiant, and I was stunned. As she walked out, time slowed, and every troubling thought and disappointment fell away.

Topher and I share a love for music. Her family loved to sing a lot more than mine did. For her Kuhingira ceremony, her brothers and cousins had composed farewell songs to let her know how much they would miss her, and to wish God's blessing in her marriage. After the opening hymn, they came out and performed these songs in full harmony.

My father-in-law's faith was fanned into flame during the East African Revival, and in the tradition of a dedicated evangelist, he could not let an opportunity to share the Gospel pass by. The local parish priest also shared his testimony, and for about an hour the Kuhingira turned into an outdoor evangelistic meeting. The priest's powerful message told the revellers that their relationship with Jesus needed to be more than what popular tradition taught.

Finally, Samwiiri Turahi, a man of few words, stood up for his speech delivered in point form. He invited the leader of our delegation, Solomon Bekunda, to receive the bride. Marriage is not just a union between two people, but also a relationship between two families. One head of the family gives the bride to another head of the family as this symbol of unity.

By this point, I was getting overwhelmed. We had the consent and blessing of her family, and I was going to marry the woman I had loved for many years. The weight of my emotions descended upon me, an almost physical sensation that manifested as ringing in my ears, and a crushing feeling in my chest.. After the ceremony and the handover was complete, my family was invited into the house and served an enormous meal. Everyone who attended the ceremony ate a good meal, but we were served the best spread. It was made to honor our family, but also was a way to show off the cooking skills of the women in the home.

Sitting there and feeling overwhelmed by the moment, I could hardly eat. The transportation snafu earlier in the day meant we were only a handful. To boost the numbers, a few in-laws from the Turahi family, the older "Bakwe", could join us in the house. As people ate and chatted around us I sat in a hazy daze, the reality of my marriage to Topher the next day finally sinking in. It was unbelievable that without means, a checkered past was getting to marry the woman of his dreams. I had the consent and blessing of her entire family. It was almost too much to believe.

With the meal finished, Samwiiri came to our group to ask about the transportation arrangements for the next day. Topher had a group of about thirty young men and women and a few elders from the village, the Abashendekyeza, who expected transportation to and from Kambuga the next day. He said that they needed 120 shillings to hire a truck to bring them to Kabale.

The Turahi family paid for the massive kuhingira, and any other expenses for the next day were to be handled by my family. We were already 120 shillings in the hole trying to get to Kambuga. In situations like this, I would have turned to my father for the money, but he died two years before, and as a recent graduate from seminary, with no job or congregation, there was no way to find the money.

The request caught me off guard, and it must have registered on my face. Before I could blurt anything out, Solomon Bekunda, ever the diplomat and peacemaker, grabbed me by the arm to silence me, and then simply said, "Let's discuss this outside."

When we went outside, my raging emotions exploded because the request had pushed me over the edge. I was ashamed that there was no way we could afford this request. Here we were, pampered and fed more than we could eat, and we were about to turn and tell our gracious hosts that we did not have the money to transport them to Kabale. It was incredibly embarrassing and even insulting to the family.

With heavy hearts we returned to the house and Solomon told Samwiiri the embarrassing conclusion to our animated discussion. He was clearly disappointed because he had to turn away everybody tapped for the trip, but he promised to send Topher with her matron for the wedding the next day. We appreciated the gesture, but at the end of a day of celebration, as we piled into the hired car and made our way back to Kabale, crushing disappointment hung over us, a dark cloud casting an impenetrable shadow, slowly snuffing out the joy of the kuhingira.

We got back from Kambuga late on Friday, the 31st of December 1971, and I went straight to bed, exhausted from three consecutive days of travel and ceremony, and needed a little peace before the wedding ceremony. Topher's house in Bugongi was a great hideout, but the morning lay in wait laden with many challenges I was not prepared for.

I started the day by getting a trim at a barber kiosk owned by Musirimukahe, and then went to Solomon and Loy Bekunda's home close to the cathedral where the service would be held later that day. My uncles had promised to provide a couple of goats as meat for the reception, but when I got to the Bekundas' home, the goats were nowhere to be seen. I pushed down rising panic, choosing instead to hope against hope that my uncles would come through, and the goats were simply on the way. While I was getting my outfit ready, I received the news that Topher and her group had arrived and were at the home of friends of ours - James and Grace Ndyabahika. More good news arrived as well. My bestman, Benoni Ogwal and his wife Alice had been seen in Kabale the evening before. I was eager for news of their arrival, since neither were Bakiga from our corner of the country.

As the morning progressed, I felt confident about the day, with a deep sense of comfort that things were taking shape. I got dressed and made my way from Solomon and Loy's home to the cathedral to get ready for the wedding service, scheduled for 10.00 am.

On the way to the cathedral, I was told that the goats would not be delivered. I could not believe it. My father's brothers let me down, knowing how high the stakes were. For the second time during the entire process, our family was going to be an embarrassment especially after the lavish celebration at the Kuhingyira. No money to transport Topher's entourage to the wedding, and now we couldn't give them a decent meal at the reception. I honestly did not know how we were going to work it out.

By the time I got to the cathedral, frustration, and sadness had bowed my head. My best man stood at the front with two other clergy, Reverend Canon Eliya Ndyanabo and Reverend Ephraim Mugisha. Decked in beautiful liturgical robes, they stood near the altar, ready to start the ceremony. My mother and her three sisters sat on the right side at the front of the church, and other members of our family sat sprinkled in the pews around and behind them.

The long walk down the centre aisle of St Peter's Cathedral, Rugarama stretched like a never ending road, each step marking my heart's descent into despair. I couldn't see a way out of the predicament we found ourselves in, and I was desperate that the poverty of our hospitality would not shame our clan. The report Topher's entourage took back to Kambuga would emphasize our poverty. The Baheesi are a proud clan, and this was not our best showing. My uncles' betrayal accentuated my father's absence and my heart ached. I missed him terribly. He'd have found solutions to the hospitality roadblocks we encountered. This was supposed to be a happy day, but my heart wrestled with dark thoughts and conflicting emotions. I couldn't confide in my best man to relieve the burden I carried. He too was a guest of our family in a foreign part of the country.

I stood at the front of the church, emotions running rampant through my mind and twisting my soul into a tight knot. Canon Ndyanabo received word of Topher's arrival and invited us to stand and sing the processional hymn. Not even the promise of seeing my beautiful bride striding towards me, our amazing life together filled with years of joy and happiness, could lift my head from my chest. My eyes stayed glued to the floor while I wrestled to keep every bubbling feeling from exploding. I swallowed hard to release the ball of tension in my throat and looked up when she finally stood next to me.

The few members of Topher's family that could make the trek to Kabale occupied the left side of the church. In the Anglican Church, the father of the bride gives her hand to the priest, who places her hand in the groom's. Topher's brother, Stephen, represented his father in that moment, who hadn't travelled for the service. It was fitting that he gave her away because he'd introduced us many years before. That morning Stephen could not find the courage to do it, instead remaining in his seat, eyes fixed firmly at the ground beneath his feet. Canon Ndyanabo sensed his reluctance and surreptitiously signalled to Topher's older cousin, Yosamu Kanyonyozi. Yosamu is a loud and gregarious character who glories in the spotlight. He stepped into Stephen's shoes as though that had been the plan all along, took Joy's hand and placed it in Canon Ndyanabo's hand, who gave it to me.

Canon Ndyanabo led us through our vows. When we got to the ring exchange, the sheer force of my excitement, and a heart overflowing with love, lifted the shroud of my earlier disappointment. Topher's ring was forged from metal alloy I purchased at the Kabale bookshop months earlier. The rings were blessed and Topher placed my ring on my finger. When it was my turn, I fumbled around and grabbed her right hand instead of her left. Like I said, the disappointment of the reception feast, as well as the complicated feelings of excitement and worry a man feels at his wedding stole every bit of sense from my brain. She squeezed my hand very hard, snapping me out of the tumult of emotions and confusion. I took her left hand instead, hoping no one noticed. I'm pretty sure some hawk-eyed relative did.

As the service proceeded through the end of the vows and onto the sermon, the sensation of floating above it all, of being present but viewing the ceremony through the haze of my shame, overshadowed the sermon. I felt haunted by the vision of hungry Bashendekyeza, filing into a room with empty plates while me and my family stood around empty-handed. I do not remember what they said during Canon Ndyanabo's sermon. While he preached, someone snuck up behind me and told me that one of my brothers-in-law saw my plight and bought a goat for the reception. It was dressed, was cooking, and would be ready in time for the meal.

The sermon ended, and they invited us to the altar to sign the wedding registration book and our marriage certificate. Canon Ndyanabo pronounced us husband and wife in front of our family and witnesses, and with that we sang a recessional hymn and walked down the long aisle to begin our life together.

My uncles weren't the only ones who disappointed us. The photographer I booked didn't show up. My best man's wife, Alice, and my eight-year-old nephew, Jedidah Arthur Musimenta, had cameras. We filled our wedding album with the photographs he took using his father's box viewfinder camera.

Topher and I reserved the dining hall of Kigezi High School to hold our wedding reception. Nothing elaborate was planned simply because we didn't have enough money, and with the food disappointment it turned out to be a pretty modest celebration. We served obushera for drinks, and a few important and invited guests unfamiliar with the beverage got sodas. It warmed my heart to see how many people from both our families stepped in to fill the gaps left by people we'd relied on.

As is customary at Ugandan weddings, both families gave speeches. The representative from the Turahi family, the Katerarume, spoke first. Then it was my turn. My speech was simple, divided into three parts. I thanked God for the miracle everyone was witnessing. To know my story, where I'd been and the journey it took me to get to that room beside the girl of my dreams, was to understand that the Lord had performed a miracle for them to see. Secondly, I thanked my parents-in-law for raising such an amazing young woman, and my wife for marrying me despite all the mistakes and wrong turns I'd made.

The last part of my speech followed in the tradition of my father and his fathers before him; naming my bride. The name I chose helped the gathered understand my feelings towards Topher and the place she'd taken in my life. I called her Akachuramutima, and as soon as I said her name our guests understood its meaning and laughed uproariously, clapping with the vigour the Bakiga are known for. It's tongue-in-cheek, but encapsulates my feelings towards her and exactly what was happening in my heart.

To this day I am still amazed Topher agreed to marry me. I was poor. Really poor. I had one pair of dress trousers, one button-down shirt, one coat, and one pair of shoes, which I wore the day I married her. I had no bed or mattress or house to take my new bride. She bought me a pair of sheets when I was at Bishop Tucker because she saw the state of my room when she visited and took pity on me. She was employed and doing well for herself, and her friends and colleagues at the Ministry of Agriculture advised her against marrying me, a man with no prospects on the horizon. For reasons we still don't know, I was blacklisted among the clergy and diocesan hierarchy, and did not have a good reputation in Kabale town from my days as a notorious drunk just a few years prior.

With no guarantees for a job and no path towards a viable future, she still saw potential in me and agreed to be my partner, my best friend, and my wife. Standing there before our family and friends as the most unlikely person to get married, I did not know the journey behind me would pale compared to the journey still ahead.

January 1st, 1971, Kabale, Uganda.

7

Unlikely Elevation

Exams, preparing for my move back to Kabale, as well as my wedding to Topher, filled my last months at Bishop Tucker. The Diocese of Kigezi, headquartered in Kabale, sent me to seminary and I expected to receive an assignment to a parish after graduation.

A few weeks before I graduated, I was told to report to the Principal's office. The Archdeacon of Kigezi, Reverend Canon Shem Ndimbirwe was waiting for me, a troubling notion. I met him as a student at Kinyasano Junior School, a tall man who commanded the respect of the parish priest and religious leaders all over the diocese. When we first met, he was the Rural Dean of the diocese, but I had sporadic contact with him after that. He sat with the Principal and the Secretary to the Principal. They invited me to take a seat next to the secretary.

In Uganda we have a culture of extreme deference to people in positions of authority. Being in the room with these three important people, I had to adopt a posture of deference, respect and humility.

He reached out a hand and greeted me in the long traditional greeting of the Bakiga,

Him: Kije

Me: Kije

Him: Buhooro?

Me: Mmmm

Him: Buhorogye?

Me: Mmmm

Him: Agandi?

Me: Nimarungi.

He invited me to take a seat, and I tried sitting in the most humble and deferential way I could muster.

"The Bishop sent me to tell you, we will not ordain you as a deacon next month after graduation."

My jaw nearly hit the floor. In five years at Bishop Tucker I had cleaned up my act, worked hard at my studies, and not slacked off like I had done as a teenager. As one of the older students, I knew this was the second chance that doesn't come around often. I could not believe that all the hard work would not amount to anything. I felt like a sledgehammer had hit me, but I did my best to keep my composure. As calmly as I could, I asked him why they had made this decision.

"The bishop will not ordain you because he does not have a parish to send you to right after ordination."

Graduation from Bishop Tucker was contingent on your ordination after your final examinations. They called it "The Finalists List". We said our goodbyes, my heart and mind in turmoil. They would not ordain me. I would not be on The Finalists List.

I often wondered what influenced this decision. Why would the bishop wait five years to tell me I was ineligible for leadership at a parish? Most students went to Bishop Tucker College for three years, but I spent five years getting a second-tier diploma. There was enough time to let me know what they were thinking. I felt very confused.

I suspect my unorthodox path to theological college is the culprit. In my ignorance, I circumnavigated three initial phases of the interview and recommendation processes, going directly to the bishop, asking to start the path to ordination. My audaciousness and a lack of due diligence on their part gave me a full-ride scholarship to seminary. While I was there, stories about me reached their ears. Maybe they found out I'd been a shabby and desperate alcoholic living on the streets of Kabale.

The miracle that changed my life was clear to me, and to everybody that knew me as an alcoholic street person. The people in leadership at the Diocese on Rugarama hill did not know about my rapid and remarkable transformation. It's entirely possible they developed a distasteful opinion of me as they learned my backstory. If I'm being honest, it was a minor miracle that I ended up at Bishop Tucker. I was not the person they normally sent to seminary. They would have disqualified me in the preliminary recommendation rounds.

In addition to my checkered past, my relationship to Topher may have influenced their decision. The first time she came to see me at the college, I decided we would not have a clandestine relationship and sneak around to see each other. Like my unorthodox entry into Bishop Tucker, my relationship with Topher was out of the norm.

While I was there, the college was heavily influenced by the "Balokole", a conservative group of Christians formed during the East African Revival. We knew them for their evangelical teaching and strict moral code. Their influence on the college created an unwritten rule: If you wanted to get married, you had to "walk in the light". You approached the elders of the fellowship and told them you wanted to get married. The elders would recommend a suitable girl from the fellowship to you. There was little contact between the two except for a few supervised visits till your eventual wedding.

Topher and I did not follow any of these rules because we did not know about them. She visited me at Bishop Tucker, and I went to Entebbe to visit her. People saw us walking around Kabale, holding hands during the school holiday. This was scandalous behaviour, but for whatever reason, nobody confronted me. We lived our relationship out in the open, and I figured I had nothing to hide that would cause any trouble. Upon reflection, I can see how my relationship with Topher, coupled with the stories of my past, conspired against me in the last months leading up to graduation.

A future without ordination was deeply troubling, but the bright spot of our prospective marriage was the saving grace that kept me looking forward. I focused my energy on my upcoming marriage and the life I hoped to build with Topher.

After this disappointing conversation, I received word that a muzungu on campus was looking for me. Reverend Jurgen Kanz from Germany was the head of the youth ministry at the Head Office of the Church of Uganda. We met at Nabugabo and shared a pleasant conversation at a Makerere University students camp he organized.

After we caught up, like a true German, he got straight to the point. He asked if I would like to work with him at the Provincial Youth Department based in Namirembe.

Having only just received the news that my sending diocese would not ordain me, I walked him through everything that had transpired. I told him that plans were already in motion for my upcoming marriage on 1st January 1972.

We had a long conversation that day. He wanted to hear my story and get a full grasp of the events in my past in order to understand where I was at, and what I hoped for my future. When our conversation ended, he said he would write to the Bishop of Kigezi to ask for my release to the provincial offices. Reverend Kanz also introduced me to the Provincial Youth Committee, whose chairman at the time was Cyprian Bamwoze.

The Bishop of Kigezi responded quickly after Jurgen's request to say if he was okay with hiring me as a lay person and not ordained. He had no objection. They granted me two weeks leave to return to Kabale, have my wedding, and return to Kampala, employed by the Youth Department. Topher could get a quick release from her job in Kabale and find a transfer closer to Kampala.

Two weeks after our wedding, Topher and I gathered the few gifts we received, her suitcases, and we left Kabale for Kampala to start my new job. Even with no worldly possessions, save for the threadbare clothes on my back, my excitement soared at the new journey ahead as the Provincial Youth Trainer, under the supervision of a man who took a chance on me.

✝

My responsibilities at the Youth Department were many. I provided support for Reverend Kanz, reported to the Youth Department Committee, and trained regional and diocesan ministers to lead youth groups in their local communities. All this training required a lot of travel, so they gave me a car, my first car. A white Volkswagen 1200cc Beetle whose registration I still remember! UVG 868. They delivered it to the house that the department rented on our behalf, but unfortunately no one bothered to find out if Topher or I could drive. As we looked at the brand new car neither of us could use, our house filled with lots of joyous and confused laughter. Driving lessons were in our future.

Being such a country boy, it took several months before I felt ready enough to take the driving test. With time my confidence grew and I passed, showing my driver's licence to whoever asked. Now I was free to travel wherever they sent me, extending my ministry outside Uganda, to Rwanda, Burundi, and eastern Zaire (Democratic Republic of the Congo).

On these trips I was introduced to parts of East and Central Africa I'd never thought to visit. The youth leaders we trained got to travel with me, expanding their minds to the situations of far-flung communities, and encouraging creative solutions for the problems of their home communities. We even got to fly to Mombasa, my first time on a plane, rushing to get ahead of the rest of the team to plan for the retreat and prepare for their arrival. The others had to travel by bus, but my wife and young daughters (we had two by this time) drove our faithful VW Beetle all the way to the coast.

Sometimes Jurgen travelled with me, insisting on taking the wheel. He was a more experienced driver and probably felt more comfortable in control of the vehicle, rather than in my inexperienced hands.

He wasn't wrong. I didn't understand the finer details of driving, treading heavily on the accelerator, taking wild turns as I swivelled the wheel left and right, occasionally remembering there were brakes I could apply to slow down a little. My first mishap happened on Hoima Road, a few kilometers after Kasubi trading centre.

I thought the arithmetic I'd learned in school was enough to help me estimate the speed of other cars around me. I weaved in and out of the lanes, and until that point, was successful in navigating the traffic. One day I got impatient with the car ahead of me and overtook it. There was oncoming traffic, but I thought I'd have enough time to squeeze past before the speeding vehicle in the other lane reached us. The narrow road and low power of the Beetle barely got me through the tightening space between the cars, and I scraped the side of the vehicle going in the opposite direction. Thankfully, we emerged with only superficial damage.

On another occasion, I was speeding through the hills of Kigezi on dirt or marram roads. The two-part trip started in Kampala, paused after 417 KM in Karujanga for a visit with my mother, then raced on another 150 KM to see Topher's parents. The roads at this elevation creep against the mountains, twisting and turning against the foothills. Topher and I noted the dryness of the marram road, whose heavy traffic had loosened the surface with pebbles, making every sharp turn an adventure in speed racing.

In my inexperience, I approached one corner faster than I should have. Realizing we were going too fast, I slammed on the brakes, sending the car into a zigzag tailspin. We hit the dirt mount on the side of the road and flipped over, and the car overturned. A group of men standing nearby saw the whole thing happen and ran to check on us, fearing we might be dead. When they got to us, we were pulling ourselves headfirst out of the car. Miraculously, we emerged unhurt. They checked us to make sure we were fine and helped us flip the car back onto its wheels. The VW beetle, being such a simple car, started right up when I turned the key in the ignition, and after a few thank you's, and a small gift of money to the group, we resumed our journey to Kambuga.

The shock slowly wore off as we climbed the big hill to Kerere, and as it did, Topher and I burst into song. We were grateful for God's protection, that we emerged unscathed, and amazed that people were there to help us. After this accident I became a cautious driver, refusing to take risks no matter how small they were.

When my job at the Provincial Youth Department started, Uganda was in the middle of rapid social change. The province of the Church of Uganda did not just serve parishes in Uganda, but also in Rwanda, Burundi and Eastern Zaire (referred to at the time as "Boga Zaire"). For many emerging generations, subsistence farming did not support aspirations for a better future, or for families who expected large contributions for their own needs. This precipitated a massive rural-to-urban migration as people sought better-paying employment.

People we worked with started popping up in urban centers, cementing two serious problems. First, it hollowed the labour in the rural areas out, leaving farms without workers, unable to sustain the people depending on food from their farms, also destroying the economies that relied on them.

Second, the promise of lucrative jobs with easy money in urban centers was a lie. There weren't enough jobs to absorb the influx of young people from rural areas, making criminal activity an easy cop-out occupation of their time. They turned into pickpockets, and robbers, finding unsuspecting travellers to steal from, or breaking into people's homes in high income neighbourhoods.

As a church based ministry, we were passionate about finding spiritual solutions for these displaced youth, but knew that without creative solutions that addressed their very real and practical needs, the problem would crest and explode. We created formalized programs based on traditional skills to assure employment.

We approached researchers and asked them to share their newly developed agricultural methods for lucrative farming. Some of the youth just needed to understand how to move their farming from subsistence to cash-crops. A pilot program started in the Diocese of Kigezi under Christian Rural Services, becoming the crutch on which we depended. They had outstanding success with their youth, creating a pipeline of vegetables that sold to supply chains serving Kabale, Mbarara, and even as far east as Masaka and Kampala.

In the late 60s and early 70s, Uganda opened more destinations for tourism. A thriving industry of crafts and souvenirs grew alongside tourism, prompting us to develop a two-pronged strategy to help youth willing to enter this market. First, apprenticeship programs to learn the art of craft creation, and the second was to create a central depot to purchase the crafts and distribute them to the markets tourists frequented. The youth offices were centrally located, and acted as a conduit for the souvenirs, making it unnecessary for the youth to leave their villages because they could get paid without leaving home. We created a pseudo cooperative that was the go-between for the youth and the craft markets they supplied.

There was a need to capitalize on the rich cultural and music heritage of the tribes in the country. Uganda is at the intersection point of four ethnic groups: Bantu, Nilotes, Hamites and Nilo-Hamites. There are many tribes with distinct languages and traditions, contributing to an incredibly rich history of music, drama and dance. To this day, music, drama and dance are popular mediums for entertainment, satire, cultural commentary, and education. If we carefully curated and cultivated these disciplines in the Youth Department, we could divert their energy towards constructive paths to make them income generators for their communities.

We focused on encouraging this artistic entrepreneurship through music in churches and faced incredible pushback as we navigated this unknown minefield. When missionaries planted Christianity in East and Central Africa, they discouraged many tribes from bringing local instruments into worship services. They claimed repurposing instruments used in local shrines for the worship of local deities was contrary to congregational worship. It was a controversial colonial sentiment, but stuck to the church culture, making local instruments absent in worship services. This was particularly true of churches in urban centres. With the rise of staunch conservatives in congregations, and the growing sophistication of educated people in urban centres, they discarded local instruments in favour of pipe organs and pianos.

Many young people were initially resistant to the idea of music or drama inspired by their local heritage and wanted to focus more on creating music with western instruments. It was an uphill task trying to convince them that local music instruments in and of themselves were not evil, and could be used, just like the imported ones, in worship services. We spent many months retraining their minds to help them see this, and the scripture that had the greatest effect was Psalm 150.

¹ Praise the Lord.

Praise God in his sanctuary;

praise him in his mighty heavens.

² Praise him for his acts of power;

praise him for his surpassing greatness.

³ Praise him with the sounding of the trumpet,

praise him with the harp and lyre,

⁴ praise him with timbrel and dancing,

praise him with the strings and pipe,

⁵ praise him with the clash of cymbals,

praise him with resounding cymbals.

⁶ Let everything that has breath praise the Lord.

Praise the Lord.

Harps and lyres accompany Ugandan cultural singing. We use trumpets and timbrels and dance. We have strings and pipes and drums. The more that we talked about it, the more we saw change, which has lasted to this day. In rural congregations all around Uganda, you will find worship services where people use local instruments, and the youth lead, not just in singing, but also the playing instruments.

To create incentives and a focus for our work in music, we put together the very first National Youth Festival at Namirembe Cathedral, barely two years after I first started at the Youth Department. It was a massive endeavour. We invited congregations from the smallest in the province to the largest, asking them to compete in several areas. There was a handiwork competition, a music competition, a traditional dance, and a drama based on a passage of scripture. The adults from the various congregations that participated could be involved in the preparation, but could not compete at the festival.

We sent every team a song that we curated centrally, and asked them to write another song based on a passage from the Bible, or a particular faith teaching. Their composition had to draw from their local tradition, accompanied by local instruments unique to them. They disqualified any team using western instruments.

The winner of the competition got the privilege of presenting their original composition at the Sunday service at Namirembe Cathedral. Namirembe Cathedral is an imposing building. Constructed from red bricks, it sits at the top of Namirembe Hill, like a jewel in a crown, and is easily seen from all directions. Soaring arches lift worshippers to the heavens, their praises resounding in the massive domes of the ceiling. Large bells call to all who can hear them, reminding them to get ready for church. It occupies a place of lore and reverence in the history of the church of Uganda. It was one of the largest Anglican cathedrals in East and Central Africa, and many important people from the government, ministers and members of parliament, attended services there. The opportunity to perform on stage was a great honour.

On the day of the competition, it quickly became clear that some youth groups twisted the rules to give themselves an advantage by selecting choice competitors from different youth groups. After some deliberation, we let them participate as they saw fit, and in the end, were very pleased with all the submissions. It was a colourful and lively celebration that highlighted Uganda's incredible diversity. Everybody enjoyed the music, dance and drama on display.

At the back of our minds, we knew there was a problem. Namirembe Cathedral hosts a high-brow congregation. At great expense they installed the largest pipe organ in the country, and the elders of the church folded their esteemed faces into grim frowns at the very mention of traditional instruments. For many of the youth, this was their first visit to a city like Kampala, and even though they were on their best behaviour, they would dismiss any slip up as youth being unruly. Any group that strolled in with traditional drums would cause a stir, and we'd be dis-invited to any future services. Many of the teams taking part in the competition used drums, and if the winning team used drums, it was likely the church elders would quickly usher them out.

God has a sense of humour. The winning team was a youth group from Ankole diocese and faced similar issues in their preparation for the competition. They swapped their drums for clay pots, and on the morning of the presentation at the service, the church elders did not turn them away.

Archbishop Janani Luwum was the officiant of the service that morning, and after his message they invited the winning choir to the front of the cathedral. They carefully arranged themselves on the steps at the front of the cathedral that separates the choir from the congregation, took folded banana fibers out of the clay pots, and slapped the mouths of the pots. The pulsing, infectious rhythm of Ankole filled the cathedral, taking everybody by surprise. Some elders, offended by the sound of drumming, and eager to align themselves with the stance that traditional rhythms were evil, stood up and walked out in protest. The youth were unfazed, and soon people joined in, smiling, clapping, and swaying to the beat. When it was all done, Archbishop Luwum walked down the steps, a gigantic smile fixed on his broad face. He presented them with the victory shield, blessed them, and sent them on their way.

As mentioned, my work at the Youth Department involved a lot of travel that didn't just happen on the weekdays, but started encroaching on the weekends. It got so bad that my weekend stops at our home in Kampala were just long enough for me to grab a change of clothes and run off to the next training session in the next diocese. The demands of my schedule took a toll on my wife. Even though we had travelled to Kampala to build a new life together, I was an absent husband and didn't take the time to build strength into our marriage. Joyie (I had stopped calling her Topher in favour of her second second christian name) felt abandoned.

If I am being completely honest, this behaviour early in our marriage was a combination of three factors. I had never seen a healthy marriage between equals, and for much of my young adulthood, I lived a selfish life without many responsibilities. Lastly, I was flattered by the throngs of young people who clung to every word I uttered. Much of the work was directly meeting the needs of youth all over the country, and they were desperate for the material we shared, but it came at a high personal cost. It did not occur to me that I needed to consider a healthy balance between my marriage and my work.

During one of my week-long trips, Joyie separated our belongings right down to the pictures in the photo albums. It was not a tough job for her because I had little to my name. Her intent was to return to her parents' home in Kambuga, and figure out what to do next. As she packed, she waited for me to explain her departure instead of leaving the house while I was away.

Friday that week rolled around. I parked my VW beetle in the garage and entered the house. Most of the time when I returned, Joyie would be at the door waiting to receive me, take my bags, and put away the food I had bought at a roadside market on the way home.

This time, she was not there. As I carried my bags into the house, I started calling her by the name of endearment I had given her.

"Akachuramutima! Akachuramutima!"

I listened for a response, but none came. I went to the rooms on the lower level of our house, calling out to her all the while, and still didn't hear her voice. My heart started racing. I imagined her laying somewhere in the house, struck by a terrible sickness, or incapacitated, or killed by robbers. Our little girl, Jackie, was not in the house either, so there was something really wrong. We were one of the lucky few with a telephone, but not really having any close friends in Kampala. There was nobody I could call.

I walked out the front door, looked up to the sky, and ran through all the scariest scenarios my mind could conjure. As I lowered my eyes, I saw Joyie sitting in the shade of a guava tree holding Jackie in her lap and cuddling her eyes fixed to the ground. I had completely missed them when I parked the car. I ran to them and sat beside them on the grass, and as soon as Joyie looked up and our eyes met, she burst into tears.

Her tears surprised me. I could not imagine what caused them. After a little while, I asked if she would come into the house and speak to me, and she agreed. Once we got inside, she let me have it. She calmed herself down, and firmly let me know she did not marry a house.

"I did not come here to be a house girl or a servant, or come to sit around and wait on a man. I did not come here to wash his clothes, cook his food, bear his children, and watch him breeze in and out, paying little-to-no attention to his family. So, I'm going to return to my parents' home, and I have been preparing all week. I have separated our belongings, and I shall leave for Kambuga tomorrow morning."

It dismayed me that the singular focus on my work and myself had brought her to this point. It devastated me to see how my behaviour had affected her. I was blind to her loneliness and her hurt. I spent the rest of the night listening to her, trying to understand how my long absences and lack of balance had caused her pain and loneliness. By the early hours of the next morning, I had determined to do something about the state of affairs in our marriage, and I convinced Joyie to give me another chance to prove it. The first thing I did the next morning was to call my boss to let him know I would not be taking another trip because I had urgent business to focus on at home.

1974 was my third year at the Youth Department, and I realized my education did not equip me for the job they hired me to do. Even with my training in theology to serve a local parish, this work was vastly different, requiring a set of skills I was ill-equipped for. While it had an aspect of spiritual development, it also involved administration, motivational speaking, skills training, and program directing. In addition, the youth that we met on our trips were hungry for any resources to help with employment and community engagement. One of the primary ways people received skills training was through faith-based programs similar to the kind we ran. This work was outside of my skill set.

I took a month sabbatical to work with the YMCA, but realized that, even though we saw the same issues with the rural-urban migration, we focused on solving problems in completely different ways. The only option was to return to school to receive training in the areas that needed improvement.

There was no theological education higher than the second-tier diploma I had received. My only option was to write applications to universities outside Uganda. Any universities interested in having me as a student also required that I raise the funds for my tuition, travel and accommodation. An impossibility on the meagre salary of a youth worker.

One morning, in the corridor of the Archbishop's office, the Provincial Secretary, Reverend Canon Akisoferi Wesonga (who eventually became the Bishop of Mbale) invited me into his office. He knew I wanted to continue my education, and gave me papers from a college in Canada, which he asked me to read through. His proposition was that if I was interested, we would look into the possibility of sponsorship through the Church of Uganda. As I scanned the papers he shared, which turned out to be a syllabus that covered Bishop Tucker's syllabus, it shone with lots of new material which would be beneficial.

Before I could decide, I had to discuss it with Joyie. She knew I desired to further my education, but a move to Canada would mean a pretty long stretch without me. We already had two daughters by this time, Jackie and Gloria, and a third on the way. It would be tough for her with three children without my support. We agreed to a plan. I would go ahead of them and prepare a place for our family. We would write lots of letters, make occasional phone calls, and after a year, they would join me in Canada. With our plans laid out, I went back to Canon Wesonga and told him I would accept his proposition and go to study in Canada at Huron College.

In August 1975, a month after my third daughter, Rachel, was born, my family and a group of friends took me to Entebbe Airport to begin the long trip to Canada. I travelled with Reverend Erasmus

Bitarabeho and Reverend Sam Obol. They accepted Erasmus at McGill University in Montreal, while they accepted Sam and I at Huron College in London, Ontario. We flew Lufthansa Air from Entebbe to Amsterdam, and then from Amsterdam to Montreal. We left Erasmus in Montreal, took another flight to Toronto, and then travelled by road from Toronto to London.

Just like that I was a student again, full of wonder at the journey of my life, and overwhelmed with gratitude. I was in a foreign country with a completely different culture than my own, facing a hectic post-graduate schedule ahead.

There was so much that was different about life in Canada. The food was different. The seasons soared to scorching temperatures during the summer, and dropped to arctic levels, each extreme a shock to my system. Even the students at college were different. But the one thing I found refreshingly similar was the youth and teenagers. Just like Ugandan youth, they had the same voracious appetite for information, buzzed with the same zeal and enthusiasm to explore the limits of their abilities, and were susceptible to the same misguided decisions and shenanigans. I was very much at home with them, having spent the last four years working only with their counterparts in Uganda.

As part of our study, they attached us to local parishes, and because word went round that I was a youth worker back home, someone asked me to be part of the Youth Committee for the Diocese of Huron. I took to this work like a small goat that just discovered it could jump. I loved hanging out and working with them at camps. They reminded me of the camps we ran at Nabugabo. The camp we took the teenagers to was at Lake Huron, and just like the Ugandan youth, the Canadian kids were at once serious, searching for meaning in life, while also being silly and requiring much supervision.

A silly call-and-response song that we sang at these camps, that my adult children still favour to this day went like this:

Down at HCC

Not so very far off

A blue bird died

With a whooping cough,

He whooped so high

That he whooped his head

And his tail right off!

On one hand, I loved the silliness that the kids were free to run about, ask tough questions and play games. It was so different from the camps we ran at Nabugabo. The camps at HCC missed a vital ingredient we insisted on having in Nabugabo. While the youth had fun, we gave them the chance to hear the life-saving message of our risen Saviour, Jesus Christ. In Uganda it was not enough to just give the youth life skills. We had to help them understand they needed a complete transformation - body, soul and spirit.

My understanding was that I was raising youth to become missionaries. As we equipped them with life skills, it was important to include a message of transformation for their families, their schools and their communities. I mentioned this to the leaders at the diocese, but I quickly came to realize that their understanding of what it meant to be a missionary differed greatly from mine. To them, a missionary was a person they never saw, who they occasionally raised money for, and lived in a remote continent like Africa. By this narrow definition, youth were certainly not missionaries, and not always receptive to my zealous attempts to evangelize them.

Besides my work with the youth committee at the Diocese of Huron, they attached me to Christ Church, Oxford Center. Oxford Centre is a small, rural town deep in farm country, in south-western Ontario. It was a small Anglican parish that served the town and the surrounding area. I worked with the parish minister, a young deacon unable to carry out the full ministerial duties of an ordained minister, and he relied on me for that.

Being a young adult himself, he used to gather the youth in the parish on Sunday afternoons, and in the evenings, we had campfires. It was then that the teenagers and young adults asked the same questions fielded in Uganda. Because I was older, with a wife and three daughters, I answered most of the questions about sex and relationships, because they inevitably come up when you have open conversations with youth.

My assessment of the work that we did was that youth all over the world were looking for the same thing. It did not matter if they were roasting marshmallows over a fire in southern Ontario, or roasting maize over a fire in central Uganda. They want to make sense of the world into which they are emerging, and they need a compass to help guide them through the treacherous and confusing waters of adulthood. In my opinion, the leaders of the church misunderstood this, referring to "rebellious youth" every time they challenged traditional values the adults took for granted.

My life was so radically transformed through my encounter with God, and because we were running a youth group, I thought similar transformations could occur at the church. In my mind, the answer is not complicated. On one hand, youth demand openness and honesty about the World, and they refuse to accept the rules of adulthood without challenging them. It was imperative that we introduced them to a life-changing relationship with God through his Son, Jesus. But at the parish and diocesan level a resistance to our ideas stymied our progress, and they found our evangelistic fervour off-putting. To make matters worse, Sam Obol and I were seen as interfering outsiders who didn't really understand Canadians or Canadian culture.

I successfully completed my studies at Huron College, graduating with a Master's Degree in Theology. At the end of my studies, I planned to return to Uganda and continue my work in the Provincial Youth Department. Unfortunately, we watched the news with growing dismay as Uganda descended deeper and deeper into turmoil. When Idi Amin killed the much-loved Archbishop of Uganda, Janani Luwum, it threw the Church of Uganda into frantic chaos. The President falsely accused the Archbishop of harbouring guerilla fighters in the Archbishop's mansion.

Archbishop Luwum was a leading voice in criticising the excesses of the Idi Amin regime that assumed power in 1971. In 1977, Archbishop Luwum delivered a note of protest to dictator Idi Amin against the policies of arbitrary killings and unexplained disappearances. Shortly afterwards they accused the archbishop and other leading churchmen of treason.

On 16 February 1977, they arrested Luwum together with two cabinet ministers, Erinayo Wilson Oryema, and Charles Oboth Ofumbi. That same day, Idi Amin convened a rally in Kampala with the three accused present. A few other "suspects" were paraded to the podium to read "confessions" implicating the three men. They accused the archbishop of being an agent of the exiled former president Milton Obote, and for planning to stage a coup. The next day, Radio

Uganda announced that the military killed the three men when the car transporting them to an interrogation center collided with another vehicle. Radio Uganda reported that the accident occurred when the victims tried to overpower the driver to escape. When Luwum's body was released to his relatives, it was riddled with bullets. Henry Kyemba, Minister of Health in Amin's government, later wrote in his book, A State of Blood, that "The bodies were bullet-riddled."

According to testimonies wrangled out of witnesses by their own conscience, they took the victims to an army barracks, where they bullied, beat and finally shot them. Time magazine said "Some reports even had it that Amin himself had pulled the trigger", but Amin vehemently denied the charge, and said there were no first-hand witnesses. According to Vice President of Uganda Mustafa Adrisi and a Human Rights Commission, Amin's right-hand man Isaac Maliyamungu carried out the murder of Luwum and his colleagues.

Janani Luwum was survived by a widow, Mary Lawinyo Luwum and nine children. He is interred at his home village of Mucwini in Kitgum District, and recognised as a martyr by the Church of England and the Anglican Communion. His statue is among the Twentieth Century Martyrs on the front of Westminster Abbey in London.

For those of us that knew him, Archbishop Luwum's murder was a terrible blow. A well-loved leader who brought many much-needed reforms to the church of Uganda. He placed great emphasis on the education of the priests that served the dioceses and parishes around the country, and established the scholarship funds that made it possible for people like me to further their education. Faced with tyranny, he was an unabashed advocate for truth and justice. He was a hero to us all, and a cherished mentor for all who worked in close quarters with him at the provincial level.

With the situation in Uganda escalating to a fever pitch of fear mongering and turmoil, bishops fleeing the country for dear life, it became apparent that it wasn't safe for us to return home. Joyie and I made the tough decision to stay in Canada for a while and make a go of it.

After Luwum's death, there were several students like myself who ended up stranded in Canada. Fortunately, the Bishop of the Diocese of Niagara heard about our young family stranded in London, Ontario and took us in. I took a post as the Curate at St. George's Anglican Church in St. Catharines Ontario, working alongside Reverend Walter Asbil, who later became the Bishop of Niagara. Coming from a very conservative Christian background, this was the most liberal and challenging congregation I ever served.

The congregation comprised empty nesters or people with very young children. It was a middle-class congregation with many teachers, lawyers, engineers and business people. St Catharines is a small city in southern Ontario, home to beautiful lake and riverfront properties. A few of the congregants lived as retirees in these lavish homes. I found out that a few families had teenagers who never came to church on Sunday, making our weekly gatherings noticeably hollowed out among the youth and young adults.

The makeup of the congregations made them view church more like a country club, and less as a gathering of followers of Christ. Just like the effort to evangelize the youth at Huron Church Camp, they frowned upon my attempts, and even occasionally resisted.

I love my work with the youth and being deprived of that during my stint at St George's Anglican, I sorely missed working with them. Frequently I tried to start a youth group, but because it had been many years since the church had focused on the youth, or run any programs to reach them. The whole concept was foreign to the congregation and the community. In addition, the local YMCA, YWCA and Scouts ran programs that dwarfed anything I came up with, and the few teenagers I tried to invite to our events refused to come, preferring instead to go to the other city programs.

Even with my frustration at work, living in St. Catharines was good for my family. It provided a sense of normalcy and stability. We settled into a low-income housing estate in the suburbs and bought an old, brown Chevrolet Malibu station wagon. My eldest daughters, Jackie and Gloria enrolled in school, Rachel was too young for kindergarten, and we had our fourth child, my first son, Paul. Joyie also started working towards furthering her education. She set her sights on Guelph University and took remedial courses in Math, Physics and Chemistry. During this time we also applied for permanent residence in Canada, because with the situation in Uganda we were going to be in St Catharines for quite some time.

Whoever travels will eventually return home.

- Kiga Proverb

By 1978, the situation in Uganda was dire. The economy and infrastructure of the country collapsed because of years of neglect and abuse. Idi Amin and his henchmen mismanaged the booming economy of the late 60s they had inherited, and though he ruled the country with an iron fist, a growing sense of dissent took hold among the populace. The mismanagement of the country accelerated after many ministers and intellectuals fled the country in fear, following the killing of Bishop Luwum, and two government ministers, Oryema and Oboth Ofumbi.

Things came to a head in November 1978 when troops loyal to the vice president, General Mustafa Adrisi, mutinied. Amin sent troops to stamp it out, but some escaped and fled across the Tanzanian border for safety. Amin accused the Tanzanian president, Julius Nyerere, of waging war against Uganda, and retaliated by ordering the invasion of Tanzanian territory. He was successful in annexing a section of Kagera in north-western Tanzania.

In January 1979, Nyerere mobilized the Tanzania People's Defence Force and counterattacked. Several groups of Ugandan exiles who united as the Uganda National Liberation Army supported him. Despite support from Muammar Gaddafi, Libya's president, they defeated Amin in April 1979 and fled the country when Kampala was captured.

After Amin's ousting, the new Archbishop of Uganda, Bishop Silvanus Wani, sent word across the diaspora inviting exiled priests to return to Uganda and be a part of the reconstruction efforts of the church following the ravages of dictatorship and war. When I received this call, I felt the pull of Uganda on my heart, and was convinced that we should return. My wife and several of our friends in St Catharines did not think it was a good idea. Against their protestations and advice, I moved my family back to Uganda, and if I am honest, even though I tried to do it with love, I strong-armed Joyie into the decision to return.

I didn't understand how much my insistence on returning to Uganda hurt Joy, one she carried for a few years. Not only was she looking forward to her experience at Guelph University, she had put her life on hold to allow me to further my education and calling with the church. In addition, we had settled in at St Catharines, and moving would be disruptive. But I had tunnel vision, convinced beyond a shadow of a doubt that returning to Uganda was the best decision, and nothing was going to change my mind.

In 1980 we said goodbye to our friends in St Catharines and Niagara, and returned to Uganda. I was full of anticipation at our return, but I misjudged how broken the country was, and how difficult our reintegration was going to be.

When we arrived at Entebbe Airport, no one was there to pick us up. The church that sent out invitations to get us to return did not have the courtesy to arrange for our transportation from the airport to the capital. They broke into many of the boxes we had travelled with and we lost some valuable clothes and toys for the children. This was just the beginning in a long line of disappointments that awaited us. Thankfully, my sister-in-law, Karen and her husband Joram were waiting for us at the airport and with their help, we found some room on the Uganda Airlines bus that took airport workers to and from Kampala.

The Uganda Airlines bus dropped us off in the bus park, and having nowhere to stay, we hired a car to take us from the bus station to the church offices. As we drove from the bus and taxi park to Namirembe, the reality of what had happened in Uganda began to settle in. Forlorn buildings in dire need of a paint job were riddled with bullet holes. The stench of decomposing bodies filled the humid air, sticking to our bodies and turning our stomachs as we drove up the hill on Nakivubo road. There are many routes to take from the bus station to the church offices, and to this day, I cannot figure out why the driver took us on the most harrowing one.

At the Church of Uganda head offices in Namirembe, nobody was waiting for us. We sent word of our travel and arrival date, were assured of a welcome reception, and yet everybody sounded surprised to find us waiting there. They had done nothing to prepare for our arrival. From all the letters and phone calls exchanged, the leadership created the impression that they were doing everything to make our arrival smooth. I thought I was returning to a job, having been promised one, and that there was a house waiting for us as there had been when I was the provincial youth worker. Standing there in the church offices, every mouth agape and no hand outstretched in help, it dawned on me. There was no job. There was no house. We were stranded. We spent the night with Karen and Joram at their home in Lungujja, a suburb of Kampala, and the next day I went back to the Church offices to see if they could do anything.

They gave us a room in a bed-and-breakfast that the church ran called Namirembe Guest House, assigned to Room 19. As I moved my family into the room at the guest house, four small walls to contain my growing family. Regret descended like a heavy blanket, stifling every breath. Had the move been too hasty? There was no turning back. We stayed in room 19 for many months to come, till management kicked us out of the room. They let us pitch some tents on the guest house grounds. With no job, I could not find accommodation for our family. We were at the mercy and good-will of the guest house managers. It was a hard season for us.

Joyie decided to see if they might accept her back at the Ministry of Animal Resources and Fisheries. She was a veterinarian with the ministry before we left, and with the hollowing out of the professional class in the late 70s, she thought there might be an opportunity to find work. To our great relief, she got her job back, easing some of the financial pressure on our family, but we were not out of the woods yet. I was still unemployed and unsure what my next move would be.

I did not have a job because the church was in disarray after the collapse of the country. Before they reinstated lower-level jobs like mine, several bishops needed to return from exile, and together they convened a series of meetings to reconstitute the dioceses across the country. The months of meetings lumbered on with no relief. Some people expressed increasing concern about my situation, with no assignments or decent accommodation. The Provincial Secretary and chief administrator said there was no funding available to pay me, keeping us in limbo. The diocesan national infrastructure was not yet reconstituted, and there were no pipelines of finances to fund the work at the national office level.

At one meeting, someone brought up my situation again, and one bishop asked if there was anyone doing the job I used to do before I left for my studies. There was no one. They did not have funding to salary the position, but there was a vacant house attached to it. They allowed us to move our family into the house while we waited for the streams of funding for the Youth Department to be reconstructed. Even though I did not have gainful employment, my family could finally move out of the tents at Namirembe guest house to a home where we could grow and flourish.

After a few more months of uncertainty, I received a call from the Head of the Youth Department, who asked for a meeting at his office. The committee in charge of Youth Affairs at the national office let me work as the Provincial Schools Chaplain. There were fourteen secondary schools under the direct chaplaincy of the national offices. Just like that, we were up and running. I had a large portfolio under my belt, and with my wife's job at the ministry, it felt like things might be looking up.

We enrolled Jackie at Buganda Road Primary School, Gloria and Rachel at Nakasero Primary School, and Paul started at Kampala Kindergarten, and Joyie was expecting our fifth child, Peter.

8

Unlikely Influence

Returning to work at the Provincial Youth Department felt like returning home to find they kept your favourite warm blanket. I had a larger portfolio and had developed many skills, but I was back to the work that kept me energized and filled with passion. The weekly interactions crackling with boundless energy and cheeky curiosity, watching lives change as the youth encountered the Saviour, and grew mighty and strong in him. This time around, the job was different. I put aside everything I learnt from my previous work with the provincial department and Canada, and came up with a brand new way to do the work I loved.

The young people differed from the ones I worked with in the early '70s. Having lived through the atrocities of war, watching as people with ill intent ravaged their country, it affected their outlook on life. I was also older, no longer the cool older brother in his late twenties and thirties. My engagement with them had to transform.

As I prayed about it, God challenged me to invite the teenagers and young adults I was working with to engage in a more intellectual-spiritual formation process. In addition, God led me to include the students at the three major tertiary institutions at the time- Makerere University, Kyambogo Teachers College, and Uganda College of Commerce, Nakawa (now Makerere University Business School). As part of the reconstruction effort that the church was elbows deep in, we needed to work with young men and women at these institutions, who would later return to their communities as professionals and leaders.

I met many young people who changed my life and taught me the kinds of lessons that can only come from the youth, and two of them made the biggest impression. Benjamin Twinamaani, who is boisterous, and loves to dance. We nicknamed him Ben Twin. Abraham Owino Yeyo, with a more quiet and deliberative disposition, was the second man. The fire that blazed in their hearts for their faith was unquenchable. Their energy and enthusiasm was so infectious that we often spent countless hours in my office brainstorming ways we could have a significant, lasting impact among the youth in our country. We came up with a vision called "Uganda For Jesus," one that I pursued for many years to come.

Ben Twin received a scholarship to further his education abroad and left our little group, but Abraham, a student of Statistics at Makerere University, stayed on, and became a trusted ministry partner for many years.

One strategy of Uganda For Jesus was to recruit students from Makerere University and prepare them to serve as lay chaplains in the 14 schools I handled. We targeted students studying Education and

Public Administration because they were most likely candidates to fill teaching positions and administrative positions at schools around the country. Our idea was to build a network of leaders across secondary schools in Uganda to increase the impact of our work in the emerging generations. One of the critical components to the reconstruction of our country was raising up youth and young people whose relationship with Jesus could transform their lives.

We had the support of the leaders at St. Francis Chapel, Makerere, and with their help, we revived the young adults camps we used to run at Nabugabo. We packed three buses with students, whisked them off to the camp for a week, and spent it running a three-pronged program.

- Evangelism: To know and love Jesus, and encourage them to share the message of salvation with boldness.

- Leadership training: To understand that their status as university students elevated them in their communities, and using this influence to spark the transformation Uganda needed.

- Having fun: Enjoying the shores of the beautiful lake, swimming, playing games and leaving refreshed.

Like every new program, unforeseen circumstances complicated our initial efforts. There was only so much training we could do with the students at Makerere, who had to balance it with their own education. The second complication was that the students we trained did not disperse across the country. After the war, there was a second surge of youth into urban centres across the country, especially Kampala. With the proliferation of private schools, they snapped graduate teachers up before they could consider other options. Our national network of lay chaplains frayed like the end of a sisal rope, stretching into nothingness.

The third unforeseen challenge to our work was the Scripture Union. Archbishop Eric Sabiiti, Janani Luwum's predecessor, invited an organization from the United Kingdom called Scripture Union, to do youth work in secondary schools. In the absence of a formalized Youth Department, he outsourced the youth outreach work all over the Anglican Province of Uganda, Rwanda and Burundi to them. Scripture Union sent an English missionary to Uganda to run this ministry, and for a while was headquartered at the central offices in Namirembe.

When Eric Sabiiti retired, Janani Luwum enacted changes to the central offices, one of them being the empowerment of the Youth Department. The missionary running the Scripture Union ministry felt sidelined by these changes, and so he moved his offices out of the provincial offices to the garage in a house in Nakulabye. He rebranded Scripture Union as an interdenominational ministry separate from the Anglican Church of Uganda.

We attempted to start a working relationship with Scripture Union, but several factors thwarted our efforts. Even though the work of the Scripture Union was supported by the Anglican Church, and many of the national leaders of the Scripture union were Anglicans, the missionary entrenched the idea of interdenominationalism into the organization. They insisted on keeping things separate, resisting any efforts that we tried to make to work with secondary schools, instead seen as a threat to their work. Many churches with established ministries in secondary schools were supported by the Anglican Church, and my superiors felt that the interdenominational nature of Scripture Union was not necessarily supportive of the interests of the Anglican Church. It was a territorial dispute, plain and simple.

We convened several meetings with the leaders of Scripture Union to explore paths for collaboration, or at the very least, a peaceful coexistence. Finally, they reached a resolution. The Church of Uganda would work to reach students through the Chapels already established, and the Scripture Union would work through a patron and a student-led committee in each school.

Scripture Union taught the distinction between simply attending church - a nominal Christian, and being a committed or "born again" Christian, colloquially referred to as "saved". This distinction created enclaves of "saved" students at the schools, conducting meetings separate from the daily/weekly services run by the school chapel. After the decision to coexist, there was no operational difference. The Youth Department of the Anglican Church supported the chaplaincies at the schools, and the Scripture Union worked through the fellowships of "saved" students.

Expanding the work in schools and tertiary institutions increased my portfolio. I supported schools and figured out a way to support work at the parish level. This work was challenging. In the early to mid-80s the same rural-urban migration of the 70s started all over again. Because of the devastation of war, the economies that supported cities collapsed, and instead of trying to find legal, gainful employment, many youths found work in the darkest corners of the black market. A growing disdain for education took root, giving way to an obsession with making quick money. Smuggling was on the rise, armed robberies turned formerly safe neighbourhoods into terrorized communities, and prostitution proliferated everywhere in the city. The landscape we worked in warped and crunched under these stressors, forcing us to change our methods to match these new challenges. If we resurrected programs from the early 70s, we thought outreach at the parish level might have more success. We couldn't do it just with words, but with concrete, legal ways to change their financial circumstances. As well as reviving the apprenticeship programs, we also revived the Provincial Youth Convention.

We revived the Youth Convention in 1983, nearly 10 years after the last one. While I was in Canada, no one stepped up to ensure their continuation, and the political and social upheaval of the '70s made travel and group gatherings too dangerous. When we sent out the invitations, the response was enthusiastic, and many dioceses around Uganda responded by sending eager representation from their parishes.

Just like the early '70s, it was a three-day competition of arts and crafts. Each team focused on the specialty of their part of Uganda, bringing fine things both unique and beautiful representing their sending diocese with pride. The grand prize was an opportunity to perform at the Sunday service at St Paul's Cathedral, Namirembe, and a plaque and recognition from the Archbishop of Uganda.

Namirembe Cathedral had not changed. They were still an elitist and conservative congregation that preferred the sound of the pipe organ to the sound of drumming. Some remembered, with indignant irritation, the entire incident regarding the pots from the Ankole group, so they gave us the same instructions; under no circumstances were we to bring any drums (or drum substitutes) or guitars into the worship service.

The Dean of St Paul's Namirembe, Reverend Canon Yowasi Senoga was gentle, but firm as he explained the rules. I tried to push back by expressing my concern that insisting on conservatism was out of step with emerging generations, but he counselled me in Luganda saying, "Son, do not worry about these old people. They do not have long to live, and the changes you are looking for will come to this cathedral."

The winning team from Madi/West Nile Diocese accompanied their songs with a series of bow harps called adungu. Small adungu play higher register notes, medium adungu play in the midrange, and large adungu carry the bass of the tune. The base of the large adungu is also hit by a second player to provide rhythm to the music.

As the winning choir filed in, inspectors crowded in to make sure we were not breaking the rules, and found the adungu innocent enough. After the sermon, my boss, the Provincial Youth Secretary - Canon Mesach Apuuli Kinobe - stepped forward and invited the choir from West Nile Diocese to present the best original local-language composition. The youth came up, carefully arranged themselves at the front of the stage, tuned their instruments, and launched into their song. The sound of their adungu and singing filled the cathedral, and the low-end bass sounds from the bass adungu filled out the bottom end of the sound, providing rhythm and bass. Once again, some elders stood up and walked out in protest. God had a sense of humour and was speaking back then about the change coming to Namirembe.

As I write this book, the English service at St Paul's Cathedral Namirembe enjoys praise and worship using the pipe organ, young people lead worship using drums, guitars, keyboards, and even brass instruments. The very thing they fought so hard to keep out of those elite walls has become a source of life for emerging generations in that congregation, and will be a sustaining force.

The 1983 convention was unique as a celebration of the cultures making up the Anglican Communion in Uganda, but also was a turning point for the leaders at the provincial youth level who chose to make decisions to impact future work within the Youth Department. They made two resolutions:

1. To ask the Church of Uganda to rename the youth ministry as the Anglican Youth Fellowship. During Idi Amin's regime, they banned all Christian denominations except the Anglican and Catholic national churches. After they ousted him, there was a concerted attempt to reconstitute banned denominations, each claiming to be the one true church of Uganda. The leaders of the convention came up with a name as a clear identifier of the work happening under the Provincial Youth Department.

    A desire blossomed within the youth for an intentional cohesion at the national level. Even though they originated from different dioceses, they did not consider themselves as separate youth fellowships, but as one national fellowship, and insisted on being referred to as one. The word "fellowship" was a compromise. They originally chose "movement" to show that they belonged to a spiritual move of God within the Anglican Church in Uganda. In 1981 a dispute about the elections erupted, resulting in a rebel movement led by Yoweri Kaguta Museveni called the National Resistance Movement. They discarded the word "movement" in favour of the word "fellowship" so there could be no misunderstanding about the intent of the youth in the Anglican communion.

2. The second resolution was a response to the need for vibrant worship across congregations all over the Church of Uganda. British missionaries planted the Anglican Church in Uganda, lugging the entire liturgy of the Church of England. Many of the first bishops and administrators of the early Anglican Church in Uganda were British, and adopted the 1662

liturgy found in "The Book Of Common Prayer". It was old and enmeshed with the culture that wrote it. Young people thought it stale and hard to relate to, and they were desperate for something more vibrant and locally produced.

Part of this resolution was a request to the Provincial Youth Department to create a choir, a catalyst to introduce renewal in worship in the whole ecclesiastical province of the Church of Uganda. This choir would carry the name of the national fellowship and be called the "Anglican Youth Fellowship Choir" or AYF. They handed the responsibility of finding and recruiting choir members to me. By this time I had cultivated a strong association with St. Francis Chapel at Makerere University, which proved to be helpful in recruiting the first members of the choir.

Ben Twin and Abraham Yeyo signed on right away, and we recruited a multi-talented musician called Stephen Yungrwoth Kasamba from Makerere University. Others came from the youth fellowship at All Saints Cathedral in Nakasero. Christine Mugwanga, a soprano with a large personality; Mirika Mubiru, an alto, an opposite personality to Christine, but became fast friends; Lillian Karamagi and Mary Humura, two soft-spoken altos; Reverend Wilberforce Serunkuma and Hannington Mutebi rounding AYF out as tenor and bass singers.

Abraham took leadership of the group. Having worked with me for over a year, he had proven himself as a leader, and participated in creating the "Uganda For Jesus" vision. With an eye for detail, and not content with half-baked creative attempts, Abraham became responsible for many of the early development of individual gifts within the group. He spent hours with another recruit, Vikki Kabali-Kaggwa, rewriting original compositions to make sure they were the best they could be. Through his leadership, we established AYF on a firm foundation it still stands on today.

Recruiting the choir and getting it up and running was more challenging than I expected, making an already overflowing portfolio even more complicated. Even though the choir directly resulted from the resolutions from the National Youth Convention, there were several problems that we immediately encountered as soon as we tried to start it up.

One of the first hurdles was finding a meeting space. All Saints Cathedral proved difficult, having to juggle numerous programs that competed for limited space. We tried meeting at Nakasero Primary School where Gloria and Rachel studied, but that too did not work out. Finally, we approached the chaplain of St. Francis Chapel, Reverend Lusania Kasamba, and asked if we could use the chapel to rehearse. One of the first people we recruited was his son, Stephen, and he agreed, and even allowed us to use one of the storage rooms to store our equipment. The chapel was a godsend because with no residences close to the building, we could practise into the wee hours of the morning, affecting no neighbours.

As the members of the choir got to know each other better, they uncovered a passion for evangelism rather than training and leading worship. It was a natural evolution for the group, because Ben Twin, Abraham, Stephen, Christine, Hannington and Wilberforce fervently yearned to share their faith. We recruited heavily among youth and young adults in Kampala, forming a multicultural group who preferred to sing and compose original songs in English rather than their own languages. This was another unforeseen, natural evolution, but it made sense because emerging generations of youth spoke English in schools, institutions and churches. They no longer referred to themselves by tribal association, but by their national identity as Ugandans.

Initially they formed as a choir, but had a greater affinity for the sounds of '80s bands than church choirs. They adopted a pseudo-rock sound, added electric guitars, keyboards, drums, and a bass guitar. They stopped calling themselves a choir, choosing instead to call the group a band.

This tridented evolution made us welcome in secondary schools and youth fellowships around the country, but it was not all good news. Some parishes and congregations resisted our presence, calling the music "noise". In particular, they did not like the drums and bass guitars. There was also confusion among the patrons and parents of the choir who had assumed AYF would represent the cultures of Uganda, and had a hard time accepting the new direction the group took. These challenges did not deter AYF, and after a few short years, they went to Nairobi and recorded and released three simultaneous albums, "Come To Me", "Beyond the Valley" and "The Visitor".

AYF leaned into their evangelistic and mission calling. They toured every corner of Uganda whether they were welcome, and the more we showed up in parishes and dioceses where we were not welcome, the more our boldness grew. We knew that had an impact among the youth even in places that didn't welcome us and started considering ourselves an insurgency group. Some in AYF even started referring to the group as bandits. During the early days, our trips were filled with equal amounts of rollicking adventure and overwhelming challenges.

At the time we started touring around Uganda, only a few bus routes could get us to remote locations, and there were very few actual buses servicing these routes. There was high demand for seats, and for a group of our size, it was an expensive and logistical challenge to reserve the number of seats we needed. It was common practice to pay a little extra to the bus conductors so they could spend the night sleeping in their seats on the bus. This was an untenable proposition with the amount of money at our disposal.

Instead of spending the night, we gathered at our home in Namirembe. At four in the morning, we sent our strongest and most assertive young men to the bus where they paid for, and commandeered the required number of seats. They spent the rest of the morning fending off other travellers till we arrived. Sometimes there was a fair amount of shoving involved to defend our seats, further cementing our self-proclaimed status as bandits.

Our trips are too many to describe in this book. I could fill a series of volumes with unexpected adventures and tough lessons we learned as we crisscrossed the country. One particular trip stands out in my mind. We wrote to the Bishop of the diocese of North Kigezi requesting an invitation. In our letter, we asked for room and board, and access to some schools and parishes that fell under their leadership. This was the standard procedure.

The Bishop responded, asking us to cancel our trip. We were not welcome, and it bothered me to no end. I was looking forward to the trip, and the Bishop was a mentor and friend. He took a personal interest in me while he was the Principal at Bishop Tucker Theological College during my years there. The more that we prayed about this trip, the more convinced we became that the Holy Spirit was calling us to go despite the letter of rejection we received. There was a clear sense that there was important work to be done in the schools the diocese served.

We came up with an alternative plan. Joy's dad lived in North Kigezi diocese, and he loved having young people in his home. We asked to use his home as a base for our outreach to schools in the diocese, and he agreed to our plan, and the entire group descended on his home for a few days. We used his contacts at his local parish to see which schools we could visit. In typical AYF fashion, we left Kampala, commandeering seats on the bus, and using the little money we had to get us there. On this trip, we did not have enough money to get us back to Kampala. We felt called, but we were unsure how to make it back. This was going to be an exercise in faith for everyone involved.

We got to Rukungiri town, 300km away from Kampala, and decided it would be inappropriate to visit the diocese without informing the Bishop. We stopped over at his house for a quick visit to let him know we would not be a strain on his home or his departments. On our way to his house, we saw a truck belonging to the diocese and flagged down the driver, told him who we were, and he bundled us into his truck and drove us to the Bishop's house. The Bishop stood in front of the house, face set in a stern mask. We exchanged greetings, he immediately asked if I received the letter asking us to stay in Kampala.

I knew they would perceive our visit as insubordination and did my best to explain our reasons for visiting as simply and politely as I could. We came despite his letter because we felt called by the Holy Spirit. We were not dismissive of his authority or leadership. As he listened, I could feel his demeanour change. Like our group of idealistic youth, he strove to live a life sensitive to the leading and guiding of the Holy Spirit. When I finished talking, he invited us to stay in Rukungiri at the local parish because he suspected that Joy's father did not have enough mattresses for a group of our size.

The truck driver took us from the bishop's home to the local parish church, and the priest who served the congregation hosted us over a cup of black tea. It was all we had for supper, because no one was ready to host a group of our size at such short notice. This change of plans was providential, and we saw God was going to surprise us for the duration of the trip. When we prayed that night, we thanked God for favour with our hosts, and split into separate rooms for the night.

Our breakfast the next morning was the same as dinner, a cup of black tea. We set up the equipment to make sure it was still working after the rough road to Rukungiri, which included a 10-channel Dynacord mixer amplifier, and two Dynacord speakers built to survive rough handling. But twelve hours strapped to the top of a bus bumping along a road made bumpy with rocks and loose stones will test even the best built electronics. Thankfully, our equipment worked and as the noises from our sound check swept through the sleepy town, drawing a curious crowd eager to see what the ruckus was.

One of the men who came to investigate recognized me. Mr. Kawawa was a leader in the diocese, and a successful business owner. I was happy to see him, because he was a former classmate who had wondered what happened to me after I dropped out of school. After a quick conversation to catch up with him, he asked if we had plans for lunch, and I told him we did not, what with our surprise visit to the parish. He told me to take the entire group to a restaurant in town and covered the expenses for the entire group. Having had only a cup of black tea for supper and breakfast, we received this with excitement and gratitude. It was the first of a long line of miracles that happened on this trip.

That morning, while we tested our equipment and found our bearings in Rukungiri, the diocesan youth worker was hard at work. He had gone to all the schools in the vicinity and made appointments for us to perform. They saw what we did as performance, but we saw it as evangelistic ministry. The Roman Catholic Church founded the first school at Nyakibare. The history of the expansion of Christianity in East Africa is fraught with tension, false accusations, alliances with rebel groups for the control of resources, and that history passed on from retiring priest to successor. It was a small miracle that we received permission to visit a Roman Catholic school.

When we got there, the girls were assembled and waiting with the teachers, some who were Catholic Sisters. An hour into the concert, Christine stepped forward and shared the gospel. She had been a student at a Catholic high school as a teenager, and was the best person to speak in this context, and frame the mission and message of Jesus to them. In a brief message, she challenged them to receive Christ, and make it known by boldly raising their hands. Almost all the girls raised their hands, and she led them in prayer. This was another incredible miracle. The Catholic church taught that there was no need for the message of salvation because infant baptism was enough to secure your place with God, and for the girls to respond in this manner was almost antithetical to their indoctrination. The response surprised and overwhelmed us because we expected a lot more resistance.

We ended up visiting six schools and seeing over a thousand students respond to the message of salvation. The previously reluctant Bishop allowed us to use the diocesan pickup truck as transportation for the entire week, and with every stop news got back to him about the impact we had on the students. We made progress among the youth that they had tried so hard to reach. It was beautiful to watch his skepticism about our visit transform into gratitude that we came.

During our week in North Kigezi Diocese, we received many donations from the schools and parishes we visited, and graduated from the diet of black tea to steaming meals that filled our bellies. At the end of the week we returned the diocesan pickup truck with a full tank of fuel, and we paid the bus fare for our transport back to Kampala. A week of uncertainty was transformed by following the will of the Holy Spirit to minister to his flock, and God rewarded us as we watched Him fling doors open so we could enjoy his abundance.

As the years rolled on, AYF picked up unstoppable momentum within the Provincial Youth Department. At the height of all this excitement and movement, on a sunny Friday afternoon in September of 1987, the Archbishop of Uganda, Reverend Dr. Yona Okoth, called me to his office to let me know about a new assignment he had for me. He was moving me out of the Youth Department and transferring me to Makerere University to be the chaplain of St. Francis Chapel.

His announcement left me speechless for a few minutes. After a job at the provincial level that allowed me to work with youth from all over the country, this job felt like a demotion, a step back. We were waist deep in the process of building something formidable, expanding on the "Uganda For Jesus" vision. How would my work at St. Francis Chapel ride alongside that vision? How would I continue working with and fighting for the youth and young adults? Everything within me resisted the idea, struggling against the authority of the Archbishop over me. I didn't want this. Not now.

I was in for a surprise. Through my work at St. Francis, the access to young people was greater than I could have anticipated, and the impact of that ministry would stretch much further than the work at the Provincial Youth Department. At that moment, sitting in front of the Archbishop, his proclamation bouncing around in my head, I could not see it.

9

Unlikely Assignment

My association with the young adults of AYF who studied at Makerere University gave me the opportunity to get to know St. Francis Chapel, and the community that met weekly for worship services. I developed a friendship and working partnership with Canon Elusania Ngombo Kasamba, the chaplain at Makerere during my years at the Provincial Youth Department. Through him I knew the work at St. Francis was challenging, and my initial inclination was to politely, but firmly, decline the transfer. I loved my work at the Youth Department and was not interested in pastoring any community, let alone one burdened with so many challenges.

In addition, the Archbishop gave us a very short time to decide. He talked to me on Friday evening and had asked me to let him know about our decision by Monday morning. We normally make this kind of move after much prayer and discernment, and a weekend felt too short and very rushed. Joyie and I asked the opinion of people who knew the Archbishop better than we did. Specifically, we wanted to know what his reaction would be if we declined his reassignment offer and stayed in our current assignment. Everyone we spoke to advised against rejecting the offer, saying he might perceive it as rebellion, leaving us with only one option.

Monday morning rolled around and found me dragging my heavy heart to Archbishop Yona Okoth's office. With every emaciated ounce of enthusiasm I could muster, I told him I would resign my job at the Provincial Youth Department, and go to Makerere as he had instructed. Then another bombshell hit; I had to interview with the University Council. The Chaplain at St. Francis Chapel, while occupied by an appointee of the Archbishop, was also an employee of the University. My education and work experience made me an ideal candidate, and I passed the interview without a hitch and little fanfare on my part.

My children were unhappy with the move. They enjoyed living in Namirembe, had made friends with the neighbourhood children, and some of their schoolmates lived in the area. It was a quiet and beautiful neighbourhood, and they struggled with the idea of losing all their comforts. Having had a few run-ins with the higher ups at the diocesan and provincial level, I had no choice. Watching their crushed expressions, disappointment shimmering in their eyes, I still couldn't change the inevitable wave of change about to slam into us. We had to move to Makerere.

When we moved, the University assigned the chaplain a semi-detached house at 191b Kasubi View. For over 20 years (October 1987 to January 2007), this godsend protected our family while we grew, welcomed many young souls seeking counselling and comfort, and ultimately thrived.

Prior to our move, I had been a parish priest only once, while we lived in Canada. From experience, and from watching my colleagues and cohorts, the arrival of a new parish priest is always a big deal. The community pulls together to welcome them. They clean the parish house, cook a bunch of meals, and make sure that the compound around the house is in good shape. For us, this was not the case. The house had sat vacant for six months, and though the Kasamba family left things in good shape, the house was well-used, and needed a little care before our move. In addition, the untended compound was a tangle of grass and weeds that climbed the exterior walls, becoming a haven for wildlife. When we arrived with a truckload of our belongings, not a single person came to welcome us and help us unload.

The Sunday prior, we attended the service and heard the announcement asking congregants for their help, and at the very least, expected one or two people would show up. The response was disheartening. Were we not welcome? Was this a message of rejection? Thankfully, some of the young people in AYF, who attended Makerere, knew and came to lug boxes into the house. With the help of Patrick, the teenage new neighbour we moved in.

Later that week as I settled into the job, I ran into a member of the congregation at St. Francis chapel who we knew well from a fellowship, the Namirembe "Revival Fellowship". Confused about the lack of reception at our new home, I asked her about it. She laughed at our confusion saying, "In Makerere, everybody minds their own business."

This obvious message showed that this parish appointment was about to be unlike anything we had witnessed in our work in Uganda. If we were going to survive in Makerere, the members of the congregation would not interrupt their busy lives to tend to the needs of the new chaplain and his family. We had to hit the ground running if we were going to survive.

The following Sunday, the congregation invited us to a special meal after the service. The congregation put it together in the mess of one of the University halls of residence, where they planned a small handover ceremony. It was an informal and casual ritual in which they handed the key ring with all 25 chapel keys from one chaplain to another. In the six months between Canon Kasamba's departure and my appointment, the church was under the interim leadership of Dr. Canon Eustace Rutiba. Canon Rutiba and I attended Bishop Tucker at the same time. He pursued his education, achieving a doctorate in religious studies and at the time of my appointment, was a university lecturer. I was glad to see him, and considered him a friend, but during the handover ceremony, in his address to the gathered community, he said something we had difficulty parsing. "Now that you have a Pentecostal chaplain, I hope you can settle down and serve the Lord."

It seems like a completely innocuous statement, but being branded a Pentecostal in public was an indirect way of calling me a troublemaker. In the late '80s Pentecostal denominations and unaffiliated congregations made huge inroads into the Protestant sect, previously dominated by the Anglican Church. With charismatic and expressive weekly services, they threatened the much more conservative Anglican Church, who viewed them as illegitimate.

To be called a Pentecostal in Anglican circles surreptitiously implied that you were not working in the best interests of the Anglican Church or the congregation; a Trojan horse sent to destroy the congregation from inside. It also implied that your leadership was illegitimate.

I still choose to believe Canon Rutiba was joking. Most who know me understand that because of my radical transformation from a street-bound drunk to a member of the clergy, I speak about my faith with power and conviction. I'm an expressive worshipper who loves to infuse Anglican liturgy with joy and emotion. I'm also known for my commitment to the growth and impact of the Anglican Church, and always worked in submission to my bishops and leadership, at the diocesan and provincial levels. Despite the levity it attempted to produce, it was an ill-advised, off-hand comment that coloured my early days at Makerere, and I sorely wished he had not said it in front of all these people.

I immediately went into damage control, assuring the leaders, and the community gathered that I really was an Anglican priest called to serve them. I shared my testimony about being rescued from the streets of Kabale and how my journey took me all the way to Canada and brought me back to Uganda. I told them about a season in Canada when I cried out to God to empower me for his work and felt God respond by baptising me in the Holy Spirit. I told them about my journey into youth ministry and how it turned out to be some of the most empowering and fulfilling work I had ever done. I told them about the fact that the Archbishop himself sent me to them, and surely he wouldn't have sent an imposter to destroy them, would he? Of course not.

When I finished speaking, Canon Rutiba handed me the large key chain with all 25 keys that opened all the doors and cupboards in the chapel, and said I was going to have to figure them all out. He also promised to assist whenever I needed it. And just like that, I was the new chaplain of St. Francis.

The job at St. Francis Chapel promised to be a challenging assignment, but nothing in my training or experience could have prepared me for what I was about to face. We inherited a congregation with deep divisions that were not obvious from the surface, and bridging them would be long and arduous.

The most consequential rift occurred among the elders of the church. Deep disagreements festered between the students and university staff about the structure of the church, and how the affairs of the chapel were run. The University entrusted the chapel with a decent annual monetary donation annually and served as a breeding ground for many vehement disagreements.

Some advocated for the church to be incorporated and run as a limited liability company (LLC), where the Chaplain served as the Managing Director, and the Chapel Council as the corporate structure below him. They viewed this model with deep suspicion because it lacked sufficient transparency necessary for a donation-run organization.

The alternative was a traditional approach where the Chaplain provided spiritual leadership and chaired a council of volunteers. The congregation would elect this council and serve as stewards of the donated resources, provide accountability and transparency, and consult with the chaplain on matters of vision and planning for the future of the congregation.

The difference of opinions got worse over time, and in the months before I received my appointment to the Chapel, the now massive disagreement split them into warring factions. Each faction wrote their own constitution enshrining their leadership model and claimed it as the legitimate constitution of St. Francis Chapel.

They sent separate letters of appeal to the Archbishop, asking for his intervention. Makerere is geographically located in Namirembe

Diocese of Kampala. It has a special designation under the Archbishop's office. Some members of the congregation wanted the business of the Chapel to reflect a different reality from other congregations that did not bear that special designation. The congregation had highly educated people used to the rigors of argument and idea generation, but only exacerbated the conversations concerning congregational governance. Archbishop Okoth, who was close to his retirement, tactfully avoided the issue until he retired, which deepened the rifts between the factions.

Canon Rutiba counselled the feuding factions to adopt the model of leadership that other Anglican congregations around the country used; a church council chaired by the parish priest. He argued that since they were an Anglican Church, they could use this model until the Archbishop made a decision. His counsel cooled the raging disagreements, but they remained a festering wound, raw and unresolved because the Archbishop did not weigh in before his retirement.

The second rift of consequence I encountered early in my tenure formed in the student community. Pentecostal and non-denominational churches were very attractive, the appeal of vibrant and varied worship experiences more than what the Anglican Church offered. Still tied to the 1662 liturgy handed down by the British missionaries, the young 80s and 90s generations considered it stale and irrelevant.

To make matters worse, the leaders in these new churches spent a lot of time talking about shortcomings of the Anglican Church. They called the liturgy obscure, and the leadership weak, going as far as labelling the Anglican Churches dead. Student communities at Makerere who stayed with the Anglican Church found those conversations insulting and annoying.

Within the Anglican Church, certain groups of students thought of themselves as more than just nominal Christians. They were "Born Again". The students who went to the budding charismatic churches also called themselves "Born Again", and were skeptical of their cohorts that remained affiliated with Anglican congregations. According to them, being "Born Again" was a rejection of the Anglican conservative tradition in favour of a more charismatic expression of Christianity. This rift frequently reared its ugly head at the Scripture Union sponsored, non-denominational fellowship on Sunday evening. In the ensuing tug-of-war, the students who remained with the Anglican Church laid claim to the chapel space and blocked other students from having meetings in the chapel buildings, banishing the Scripture Union fellowship and starting their own weekly meetings.

When Joyie and I came in, they expected us to side with the students who remained true to their Anglican roots. This unspoken demand was confusing and distressing, because we could not understand how two "Born Again" Christian groups harboured so much animosity towards each other. The chapel leadership before my time had tried and failed to help the student factions.

One evening Joyie and I went to the chapel to visit the student fellowship that met on Sunday evenings. The other student fellowship met on the other side of a grassy quad in the university main hall, 75 meters away from the chapel. Both fellowships started at 8:00 PM, and both opened the windows of their respective meeting spaces to attract curious students with their music. On this evening as we walked to the chapel, we heard both student fellowships start their gatherings, a competition across the green that separated them, each getting louder as they sang the same song:

We are together again, just praising the Lord.

We are together again, in one accord!

Something good is going to happen,

Something good is in store.

We are together again, just praising the Lord.

Joyie and I turned to each other, mouths agape, suppressing incredulous laughter, and yet overwhelmed with a deep sense of sorrow. Two competing groups singing the same song proclaiming togetherness and joint purpose, but the truth could not be further from reality. We stood amid the cacophony, succumbing to laughter that did little to hide our anxiety. After the fellowship that night, we knew we had to work hard to heal the rift.

A few weeks later, we invited the different leaders to our home for tea. Joyie made her famous sandwiches to go along with the tea, and after sharing a few pleasantries, we got right down to business. To our surprise, the gentlemen leading the two groups were roommates, and taking the same course, admitted to the University in the same year. Spiritually and intellectually, they were equals.

I told them I did not consider myself as just the chaplain of St. Francis, but the spiritual leader of all protestants that came to Makerere, whether they came to St. Francis for our weekly worship services or not. The University recognized three main religious groups: Muslims, Catholics, and Protestants. There was no consideration given to the various denominations within each group. So according to them, all matters pertaining to protestant students fell under my purview. It took a bit of cajoling and prayer, but by the time the evening ended, both gentlemen agreed to work together to heal the gaping chasm in the Christian student body.

After that meeting, both communities repented for the disparaging and hurtful words they had exchanged, forgave each other, and began the process of healing the body of Christ. I commend these two young men for their leadership and willingness to work together. The next time the students sang "We are together again, just praising the Lord," they meant it.

All the drama and bickering created a poor impression in the minds of many would-be members. Many staff and students opted to worship in other churches around the city like All Saints Cathedral, Namirembe Cathedral, Kampala Pentecostal Church (now Watoto Church), and Miracle Centre Church. In addition, there were three strong churches just outside the University campus that exerted a powerful gravitational pull on the university and surrounding neighbourhoods - Redeemed Church of The Lord, Makerere Full Gospel Church, and Kampala Baptist Church. Their worship gatherings were engaging and powerful, led by smart and charismatic pastors, and swarmed with many programs for students and families alike. The longer St. Francis remained embroiled in divisive quarrels and challenges, the less attractive it appeared for anybody seeking stability and vision.

The greatest challenge we encountered in the first few years was that the weekly worship gatherings were stylistically out of step with the desires of emerging generations. We used two prayer books to guide the weekly liturgy at the chapel: The 1662 Anglican Book of Common Prayer written in Jacobean English similar to Shakespeare's novels, and an Abridged Shorter Prayer Book, written circa 1928 for the communion services and mid-week services. They used the Ancient and Modern Revised Hymnal last updated in 1956 for worship. As you filed into the service at the weekly gatherings, they handed you a prayer book and a hymnal.

These hymns and liturgies came out of revivals in the Church of England, and were revolutionary for their time. But by the late '80s and '90s, they were well worn and unremarkable in addressing new generations. To make matters worse, many clergy led the liturgy in the most boring monotone voice they could muster. It is little wonder that some felt it was for a church as modern and sophisticated as St. Francis to abandon the legacy liturgy of the Anglican Church.

This considerable pressure to abandon the prayer books and hymnals was persistent, but I took a different route and conducted a thorough analysis of the liturgy. I had used the book of common prayer for many years, starting in seminary, and was never told why we held onto it for so many years. I started my deep dive in understanding a peculiarity about the book of common prayer. Within the texts of prayers and psalms lurk small italicized words written in red lettering called rubrics. I peeled through them but found them difficult to understand Jacobean English, which isn't spoken anymore, but slowly pieced something quite startling together.

The sages who put the book of common prayer together were under the leadership and guidance of the Holy Spirit. They relied on the inspiration of the Holy Spirit to write prayers and service formats to breathe life in the gatherings of Anglicans in village churches around England. They were desperate for a move of God and wanted their congregations to seek a deeper and more meaningful connection with God through the ministry of the Trinity, the proclamation of the word, and the celebration of the Eucharist.

They did not design the rubrics to be a straightjacket for the church leadership, as a tool to release the church into a deeper engagement with God. They followed Saint Paul's admonition to sing or speak to one another with Psalms, hymns and spiritual songs, singing to God with gratitude in your heart (Ephesians 5:19, Colossians 3:16).

This discovery brought new life to my engagement with the liturgy, and it inspired me to teach the congregation about the power of our inherited liturgy. It compelled me, in later years, to challenge student interns from Bishop Tucker, to get out of the monotonous delivery of the liturgy and rediscover the inspiration of the Holy Spirit in the timeless words of the Book of Common Prayer.

This discovery also led to a few liturgical experiments. For the morning prayer, following the confession, absolution, and the Lord's prayer, the leader/minister says these words out of Psalm 51:15.

Minister: O Lord, open thou our lips;

People: And our mouth shall shew forth thy praise.

Minister: O God, make speed to save us;

People: O Lord, make haste to help us.

All stand.

Minister: Glory be to the Father, and to the Son: and to the Holy Ghost;

People: As it was in the beginning, is now, and ever shall be: world without end. Amen.

Minister: Praise ye the Lord;

People: The Lord's Name be praised.

This sets the stage for praise, suggesting Psalm 95, which starts with these words:

O COME, let us sing unto the Lord
Let us heartily rejoice in the strength of our salvation.
Let us come before his presence with thanksgiving:
and shew ourselves glad in him with psalms.
For the Lord is a great God:
and a great King above all gods...
O Come let us worship and fall down and kneel before the Lord
our Maker.

- Psalm 95:1-2, 6

The rubric just before Psalm 95 says, "This or any other song of praise may be sung". The writers of the rubric gave the service leader a choice for an appropriate song of praise. Rather than being rigid instructions steering us to Psalm 95, it was a suggestion. This understanding was revolutionary for me and opened doors for experimentation. Before we could truly experiment, follow-up questions emerged:

- What are songs of praise?

- What songs of praise are appropriate for our setting?

- We've heard much about praise and worship, but are they the same or different?

- How will the congregation respond to any deviation from the pre-written liturgy?

The easiest solution was to import songs from our charismatic, non-denominational neighbours, but we needed to find out if other Anglican congregations around the world tinkered with liturgy in ways we planned. I stumbled across a group of people at an Anglican Renewal conference put together by an organization called "Sharing Of Ministries Abroad" or SOMA.

SOMA was the brainchild of people from disparate Anglican backgrounds who felt that it served better the global Anglican communion to exploit the global information highway to share strengths. The challenges and opportunities in the Anglican Church could be charted by international collaboration as parishes, dioceses and provinces shared knowledge and resources. In the coming years at St. Francis, we benefited from SOMA's teaching and training of contemporary worship and its place in Anglican liturgy.

At this conference, I became convinced that God was calling us to chart a new path, and breathe life into the liturgy. With the help of the conference facilitators, I saw a path forward for St. Francis, even when I knew that unknown challenges lurked in many corners waiting to pounce and upset any forward movement.

The Chapel Council held a powerful sway over the congregation and was only marginally responsive to the leadership or spiritual guidance of the Chaplain. Attending church was a matter of tradition rather than a place where their relationship with God was enriched, or a desire to expand God's Kingdom on Earth. Most were University staff that functioned more like a council running the affairs of a social club, instead of the leading of a congregation on a shared mission, partly because the Chapel had a narrow view of its function at the university.

The changes I wanted required restructuring the Chapel Council who had to share my evangelistic vision for the future of the community and congregation. In addition, they served a multi-pronged role:

- As a check and balance for the Chaplain,
- As champions for the vision and mission that God was going to guide us to.

- To come under the spiritual guidance of the Chaplain and release the perpetual power struggle.

- To be a spiritually sensitive group, willing to seek God's direction.

With a little convincing, we started a study of leadership in the church. We focused on the characteristics of leaders in the first century church, the prototype we looked to when we needed to make sense of God's direction. In addition, we teased out the responsibilities of the leaders, to understand what function the Chapel Council had alongside the Chaplain. Our journey took us from the Gospels, through the Acts of the Apostles, and deep into Paul's New Testament epistles.

In Acts 6, the elected leaders of the congregation are:

- Full of the Spirit and wisdom. (Acts 6:2).

- A man full of faith and of the Holy Spirit. (Acts 6:5)

In Titus 1: 6-7 a leader is:

- … blameless, faithful to his wife, a man whose children believe and are not open to the charge of being wild and disobedient. Since an overseer manages God's household, he must be blameless—not overbearing, not quick-tempered, not given to drunkenness, not violent, not pursuing dishonest gain.

In the third chapter of Paul's letter to Timothy, his instructions are to find leaders with very specific qualities:

Now the overseer is to be above reproach, faithful to his wife, temperate, self-controlled, respectable, hospitable, and able to teach.... They must first be tested; and then if there is nothing against them, let them serve as deacons.

- 1 Tim 3:2, 10

As we studied these passages, we arrived at a fundamental understanding: our nomination and election process was not good. They based it on a pseudo-merit system that had very little to do with what the Bible taught. This was the main reason for the tension between the chaplain and the Chapel Council. They did not serve similar roles with respect to the mission and God's vision. The requirements for serving on the Chapel Council were so lax that they could nominate anybody, and vote them onto the Council.

The more we studied the scriptures, the more we realized the pretty high bar for leaders who served on the Council. The most important qualification was that anybody serving on the Chapel Council had to have a relationship with Christ and with the church, above and beyond simple inheritance. Something deeply personal and life-giving. In plain Ugandan Christian-Speak, any leader serving on the Church Council had to be a born-again Christian whose testimony was known to the congregation.

It makes sense that the writers of the Bible created such high standards for elected leaders in the church. The vision to expand God's kingdom is audacious, with a huge scope, that you cannot embark on biblical leadership if your faith, vision, and life do not show that you trust God with your personal life. We needed eyes of faith in order to see the opportunity in the chapel at Makerere University, an impossibility if that faith does not exist.

I was in uncharted waters wading through work tremendously different from anything I had done at the Provincial Youth Department. I sought God's guidance for the journey ahead, spending many days in the chapel gallery by myself. There was no one in the church during the week, save for the poorly attended mid-week service, and occasional check-ins by the chapel verger. After months of prayer and agonizing, I felt led to a surprising scripture that became my governing scripture:

This is the word of the Lord to Zerubbabel: 'Not by might nor by power, but by my Spirit,' says the Lord Almighty.

- Zechariah 4: 6

We had to topple the leadership structure entrenched by decades of tradition, and ask the Lord to transform a congregation trapped in the stale recitation of liturgy into Holy Spirit fire-breathers who celebrated during weekly meetings, and pulsed with the presence of God. To achieve any of these things, we had to discard the notion that we needed to wield power and might.

Surrounded by artistic interpretations of John's Revelations painted on the ceiling of the gallery, I prayed for the congregation. My eyes landed on the empty seats below, just as empty during the Sunday service. The elaborate banana fibre mosaic of the huge altar table led my eyes to the full-size cross on the east wall. I prayed the Lord would send 2000 people to attend church on Sunday. Barely 200 people sporadically showed up, the numbers trickling to devastating levels when the university students went on holiday. 2000, from 200. An audacious prayer that took over 15 years to bear fruit.

After the Bible teachings regarding elected church leadership, we convened the first Chapel Council election of my tenure. It was a dramatic affair. Against decades of practice we elected a council, tossing out suggestions based on legacy or popularity. The debate was robust and even emotional, but something remarkable started happening. Many people nominated for different offices withdrew from the running because their self-evaluation showed how unqualified they were to lead the congregation.

A variety of people comprised that first Chapel council. Some from the old cohort used their names to stand in opposition to the new guidelines, but most of the new members would lead with eyes of faith, their hearts sensitive to the leading of the Spirit. It was not perfect, but the consensus was that we no longer stewarded a social club, but a movement of people on a mission for Christ. They submitted to the leadership of Christ as the head of his church and prayerfully sought His guidance at every meeting to ensure we followed His will.

With the new Chapel Council in place, we started the hard work of asking tough questions about the congregation. We ran the chapel as a parish like any other in Uganda, but it was a specialized ministry with a unique mandate. Most parishes serve the communities in which they are planted. There are a few exceptions, of course, but generally parishes have a homogeneous representation of people from the communities it serves. St. Francis served students at Makerere University who came from all corners of the country with disparate lived experiences. It served the university lecturers who lived in and around the university campus, and it served the auxiliary university staff - the custodians, cleaners, and cooks - who not only occupied a different financial and social strata, they were also overwhelmingly "Lugbara" speaking.

St. Francis Chapel was established soon after Makerere University's commencement as part response to the religious makeup of the students. Along with St. Francis, they served three other religious groups. The population of Ugandans in and around Makerere was dominated by three major groups. St. Augustine Chapel was the catch-all for self-professing Catholics, and St. Francis for Protestants. The mosque was a present to the University from the Sultan of

Zanzibar whose son attended Makerere University. There was no place to worship or pray when he arrived, prompting his father to give the Mosque. Each of these places of worship served the staff, the students, and the auxiliary workers.

Studying the history of St. Francis forced us to ask tough questions about the chapel and its congregation. We realized that the role of the leadership stretched far beyond acting as caretakers of an institution. God was calling us to switch our focus from the maintenance of a congregation to growth through evangelism and outreach. Maintenance to mission.

Enlarge the place of your tent, stretch your tent curtains wide, do not hold back; lengthen your cords, strengthen your stakes. For you will spread out to the right and to the left; your descendants will dispossess nations and settle in their desolate cities.

- Isaiah 54: 2 - 3

Parents in the congregation who were direct recipients of the renewed vigour and focus of the leadership approached me to consider putting special focus on their children. Sunday school served Primary One to Primary Seven, and there was growing influence among university students, but existed to serve secondary school students. This critical age of spiritual development required separate attention to make sure they didn't abandon their Anglican/Christian upbringing.

The request first came to me in the second month of my chaplaincy. I was still green behind the ears, with no estimation of how truly broad the work was about to get. This request for a youth ministry caught me by surprise, but was God's way of expanding my thinking. The critical error in my assumptions about the community was ignoring the children of the staff and auxiliary staff who considered St. Francis their home church. Some children lived close enough to the university campus, had attended Sunday school, but now floated in the wind, unable to connect with the adults, and too old and awkward for Sunday School.

I focused first on Primary 7 graduates. The best way to engage them was to invite them to confirmation classes. I sent out invitations to all graduates in our vicinity, whether they had gone through confirmation. Rather than hosting regular confirmation classes, I took them on a three-month journey, teaching the fundamentals of the Christian faith, and using the Nicene Creed as the basis for my curriculum.

We started with the first fundamental line in the Nicene Creed, "I believe". This was my first opportunity to challenge them about the meaning of belief. More than just a statement to recite every week, it is a declaration of fundamental, personal truth. Declaring a belief when one does not believe makes that person a liar.

My favourite part was talking to them about the phrase, "Maker of heaven and earth", allowing me to indulge my passion for astronomy. Despite abandoning that field of study, my love for all things in the solar system and the skies above has never stopped. We traipsed through an exciting study about the universe, skipping the vast reaches of space, and bounced around galaxies. Then we delved into particle physics, and microbiology to show the wonder of the maker of heaven and earth. This detour ignited the imagination of these pre-teens, so often lost by creeping cynicism, reminding them that God made this wondrous mystery we call nature.

All things bright and beautiful

All creatures great and small

All things wise and wonderful

The Lord God made them all.

Each little flower that opens,

Each little bird that sings,

He made their glowing colors,

He made their tiny wings:

The purple-headed mountain,

The river running by,

The sunset and the morning

That brighten up the sky:

The cold wind in the winter,

The pleasant summer sun,

The ripe fruits in the garden,

He made them ev'ry one:

The tall trees in the greenwood,

The meadows where we play,

The rushes by the water

We gather ev'ry day.

The Nicene Creed provides a fundamental understanding of our faith, but before confirmation, a few questions always came up and were asked by the older children in the confirmation classes. Why go through confirmation in the first place? Where did this tradition among the Anglicans come from? Why is confirmation necessary if a person was baptised?

Besides the fundamentals, a secondary study of the origins of confirmation was imperative. Anglican confirmation is an affirmation of one's baptism by a Bishop laying his or her hands on the person seeking affirmation. This is first seen in the New Testament in Acts 8. Peter and John, the first bishops of the early church, laid their hands on Christians in Samaria who had received the baptism of John the Baptist, but had not received the baptism of the Holy Spirit.

Confirmation means more than the stuffy ceremony where a Bishop lays hands on your perfectly coiffed hair and utters the words,

"Confirm, O Lord, this your servant (insert name here) with your Holy Spirit. Empower her/him for your service; and sustain her/him all the days of her/his life."

The confirmand engages in a centuries-old tradition where the Bishop prays for the baptism of the Holy Spirit upon the individual. This is more than just catechism class, more than a sacrament passed down from antiquity. This is a sacred rite where the believer is invited into the fullness and power of the work of the Holy Spirit.

I taught that they should fully expect to be baptised in the Spirit. The Bishop, an apostle by succession and ordination, was literally like Paul and John visiting those Samaritan Christians in Acts 8.

I enjoyed my work with pre-teens and young teenagers in confirmation classes, but the work of building the youth ministry was not done. I got concerned about students in the vacation months between Senior 4 and Senior 5, and others on vacation months between Senior 6 and their first year at a tertiary institution.

Up until 1995, the education system in Uganda had a six-month vacation between senior 4 and senior 5, and an eight-month vacation between senior 6 and the first year of university. Many staff members at the university during my tenure had teenagers, just like I did, and during the vacation months after senior 4 and senior 6, they completely disengaged. Rates of unemployment soared to record numbers, massive competition for entry-level jobs ballooned, leaving many of them idle.

During a conversation with Professor Nsibambi, with daughters the same age as my children, he challenged me to start a youth program tailored to teens who faced the long months of vacation idleness. I invited two young people I had made friends with to a brainstorming meeting at my office. Dora Rukare and her cousin Gordon Kihuguru took ownership of the initiative, and invited friends to join, growing from a handful of people to over 20 young adults.

Two converging factors fueled the growth. Several youths were children of university staff living on the university campus, and St. Francis is close to the center of the city, so other youth looking for similar programs could walk or take taxis to the chapel to hang out with their cohorts.

It surprised the initial group that I did not have a name already picked out. Uganda's education system left little room for exploration and personal initiative, and they expected that I would have everything worked out. It was a deliberate choice on my part. I wanted them to take ownership of the group. Making them part of the decision-making process from the beginning ensured that they would value their creation more than a gathering supervised and controlled by an adult. I took it further, challenging them to lead and guide it in any direction they saw fit, within reason of course, and was amazed to see the natural leadership ability of the people in the group shine through as they were trusted with more and more responsibility.

As they worked out the details of their purpose, a couple of unique things emerged. They were a Christian youth group meeting weekly during the Senior 6 vacation (although they continued meeting long after). They also wanted a community that invited others from all over the city. The third was that they were not exclusively Anglican, but would open their group to youth from any denomination. Finally, they wanted their friends who were not born again to feel welcomed and find Christ through friendship and association. They called the group Come Alive.

With the establishment and success of Come Alive, students in their Senior 4 vacation clamoured for the same consideration. The same things affecting the older youth waiting for admission to tertiary institutions affected their younger counterparts. Being two years younger, I took a more direct role in the group's leadership.

I borrowed the name of a long-standing youth ministry started by David Wilkerson in 1960 and called the group "Teen Challenge". We did not have the same mandate as David Wilkerson's ministry because we were not working with youth with substance abuse problems. It was a worthy organization to emulate, because through my previous work in Canada and Uganda I saw youth everywhere struggle through the same challenges as they transitioned from teenagers to young adults.

It took the Teen Challenge program a little longer to see the big numbers Come Alive had, mostly because parents were reluctant to let their 16-year-olds out of their homes. But with every succeeding year, they saw their children were safe and engaged, and sent them to our Teen Challenge program.

Come Alive and Teen Challenge were the most successful ministry initiatives. When I left the Provincial Youth Department, I imagined my passion for youth work withering in the corner, dying a slow, painful death as the less interesting parish work consumed all my time, and was more adult-focused. Through Come Alive and Teen Challenge, I worked with thousands of youth as more parents trusted us with their children during their vacation months. In 1996 and 1997, Teen Challenge became a staggering phenomenon with regular attendance of 400 - 550 young people gathering every week. It was pandemonium, challenging, but also unbelievably rewarding.

These two ministries allowed me to develop one-on-one relationships with many of them in their formative years, and I am glad for these small moments of influence. They have become forces for good all over Uganda and the wider world. They are leaders of large companies, own successful businesses, manage public institutions, teach and educate young minds, and a great number have become church planters, church leaders, and pastors all over the World.

Capable worship leaders and musicians emerged from the youth programs. It was not an initial goal of mine, but it turns out that if you put a bunch of youth together for an extended period, they will produce music. Given the freedom to experiment, put on concerts, and write songs without the intervention or supervision of disapproving adults, their music explorations gave rise to a strong foundational group for the contemporary worship transition I had envisioned for a long time.

Our organists, Professor Paul Mugambi, Mr Lugumba, and Dr Apollo Musoke stewarded the music program before I got there, and worked with me to introduce more contemporary music into our weekly repertoire. Being classically trained, they were not enthusiastic

160

about playing songs with no written music available, requiring them to improvise or play by ear. Sam Kaddu stepped up and played the organ when they couldn't, being a hybrid musician who could both read and improvise. I owe a lot to these gentlemen, because they were willing to be stretched outside their comfort zones while we built up an emerging cohort of musicians and singers.

As new talent emerged, we transitioned to a hybrid service. All our research about liturgy, the years spent talking and musing about breathing life into the weekly services were finally paying off. This emerging group of young people could carry the vision forward.

I spent a significant portion of this last part of the book talking about worship begging the question: Why this strong focus on worship?

It comes from a very real place in my life. My life story draws a winding path from my beginnings to unfortunate calamity (and very possible ending). The path to my chaplaincy at St. Francis was exceedingly unlikely. It stumbles through complications, twisted by my pride. I staggered through the ravages of drunken youth, barely avoiding explosive events that could have ended my life. God intervened, making paths where there were none, clearing the way for my feeble footsteps. Recognizing his intervention made my faith come alive in ways that nominal Christians find excessive. The gratitude for this intervention is a continual, overflowing fountain in my heart, naturally resulting in worship. So, I share my faith, preach, and pray with passion. I sing as loudly as I can, and I dance whenever I have the opportunity. I do not hold back in worship.

James Macdonald says, "When you worship you are saying, 'This one is worth more.' At the same time you are implying, 'I am worthless.'" Worship is the magnification of God and minimizing of self. One of the most succinct expressions of worship in the entire scripture is the words of John the Baptist in the New Testament,

He must increase, but I must decrease.

- John 3:30.

Over the years I've met and argued with Christians who try to convince me that worship is more than singing. According to them, worship could be any act; cooking a meal for a disadvantaged person, helping a neighbour, or visiting the sick. These propositions disguise something deeper; for example, they don't like the emerging styles of music championed by young people. When the argument devolves into sorting semantics and minutiae, I redirect them to the more accurate definition of worship, ascribing worth to God. Faith or charitable actions may indirectly do the same thing, but the bible commands worship as our highest expression. Direct, intentional, vertical outpouring of adoration.

The best expression for worship that humanity ever created is music. Each generation invents new genres of music that sound offensive to prior generations, but music has, and will always be our best expression of adoration to God. When the writers of scripture talk about heaven, the presence, volume, and outpouring of music is ubiquitous and unavoidable. It is not just humanity's best expression; it is heaven's best expression.

This understanding made it easier to accept new genres of music youth experiment with. The first generations of Come Alive and

Teen Challenge brought electronic keyboards and guitars into our worship services. A few years later, they turned up the volume, and muscled in heart throbbing drums. They introduced the sounds of Ron Kenoly, Alvin Slaughter, Don Moen and Darlene Zschech while simultaneously jarring us with the sounds of Christafari, DC Talk and DJ Maj. I listened as they rehearsed dances, worked on harmonies, or created backing tracks on the church instruments. While it was not always my cup of tea, I was happy that these young people found new ways to do the very thing that I love.

My story also makes me passionate about helping other people meet the Lord, and watching with awe and anticipation as He completely changes the trajectory of their lives. Nothing creates an atmosphere potent with the presence and power of the Spirit of God, like a church enraptured in worship. An autopsy of every movement that saw the rapid expansion of the church through the transformation of people's lives reveals the one thing they have in common is a heart for worship.

How will anyone know that you are pleased with me and with your people unless you go with us? What else will distinguish me and your people from all the other people on the face of the earth?"

- Exodus 33:16

The distinguishing characteristic of a church overflowing with stories of changed lives is worship. It is more than the sporadic engagement of a few enthusiastic people on Sunday morning. Every leader or congregation that understands this principle has a unique and rewarding opportunity to introduce people to God in a more powerful way than simply preaching. Worship can penetrate souls and psyches, delving past inhibitions and reaching depths that prayers and elocution cannot. When people meet God in this transformative way, their story cannot remain the same. It changes so much and makes them unrecognizable.

God graced me with the privilege of watching people step away from nominal Christianity and dedicate their lives to Christ. Hundreds of people ambling along predictable paths have jackknifed before my very eyes, and I watch in awe as God writes powerful futures for those that choose to seek Him. With every transformation I raise my voice in song, lifting my hands in praise and worship, because I am reminded that my unlikely story was only possible when God interrupted a self-destructive young man and wrote a brand-new story for his life.

I am not perfect. My wife and children can attest to this. But my imperfections serve to magnify God's perfect plan. I have never held a prominent position in the church or in the private sector. I held no aspirations to those lofty offices and was too cantankerous for their politicking anyway. Nobody ever expected that the Chapel I served would be a crucible of leadership formation in the way it turned out to be. That my voice was elevated among emerging generations is a testament to the fact that God can use the most unlikely person to touch the lives of people all over the world. I am not the most eloquent speaker or writer. My lack of eloquence testifies even louder that eloquence is not high on God's list of criteria for impact or influence.

This is the word of the Lord to Zerubbabel: 'Not by might nor by power, but by my Spirit,' says the Lord Almighty.

- Zechariah 4: 6

Joyie visits Benoni and causes a stir.
Circa 1968, Bishop Tucker School of Divinity, Kampala.
(left to right, Karen, David, Benoni, and Joyie).

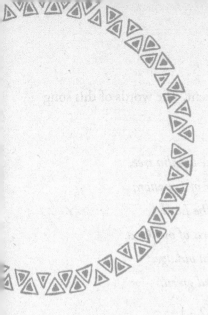

Afterword

I officially retired from active duty as an Anglican priest in January 2008, having spent over 20 years at St. Francis Chapel. My wife and I moved to Wakiso to a property Joyie bought in 1989. Wakiso is a burgeoning suburb outside Kampala that young families choose as a less-expensive location to build their first homes. It bustles with the promise of success and the excitement of young people, a far cry from the sleepy village we first encountered.

At first we did not have a clear idea what we could do with the property. We had vague notions about small subsistence farming but not much more. It took over 10 years for the vision of The Joy Center to be revealed to my wife. During that time, we fought off many protracted legal challenges to the ownership of our property, but in the end we secured it and worked towards the vision we have had.

Most people who enter retirement view it as a time to wind down and enjoy the fruit of their long years of service and labour. We felt, however, that our story was radically different. The words of this song inspired us,

The righteous will flourish like a palm tree,
they will grow like a cedar of Lebanon;
planted in the house of the Lord,
they will flourish in the courts of our God.
They will still bear fruit in old age,
they will stay fresh and green.

- Psalm 92: 12 - 14

You'll notice that the last chapter of this book ends with little story after the mid-1990s. There is a 21-year leap between the last recollections of the final chapter and this epilogue. It is not a lapse in memory or an egregious omission. Hundreds of lessons and experiences have to be carefully parsed and presented differently than the memoirs of this unlikely story.

Most people who know or recognize me are people I served at St. Francis Chapel, and they all thought they knew the complete story. The impression of me without the context of my background is incomplete. If the early story of my life remains a mystery, then my passion, my drive, my insistence on certain things makes only partial sense. This is my attempt to fill in the missing pieces so you can understand the journey that brought me to Chaplaincy at St. Francis.

You might have thought I was a conservative leader unable to change with the times, now you have a context for why I may appear that way. If you thought I was unnecessarily expressive, you understand better what fuels my expressiveness. If you felt I was unqualified for the position I held, or felt I was not ambitious enough for offices higher than the position of Chaplain of St. Francis, my guess is that you will find clues in this book to explain it.

The 20 years spent at St. Francis was the training ground for the next phase of my life, the one I am currently living through, and there are at least two more books that will come out of my experiences during those years. This was an important introduction, so you would have a glimpse into a story so unlikely, I still shake my head when I think of it.

My prayer for you is that when you finish reading this book, your heart soars with encouragement, and that once again you are in awe of God's incredible ability to change stories and histories in unimaginably creative ways.

Benoni, Joyie, and Cabbie at their home in Wakiso, Uganda. Jan 1, 2021.

Acknowledgements

Joyie:

Thank you for encouraging me to get all my thoughts out. My story is your story. I could not be the man I am without you.

Nicholas:

Thank you for your work assembling the first drafts of this book. Even though we have moved a significant distance away from your final draft, I want you to know that it would have never been possible without your effort and dedication

Paul:

You have a way with words, and I am thankful for your gift. Thank you for taking an incomplete work and fleshing it out as you did. You have made me sound articulate and interesting. No small feat at all!

Gloria and Mercy:

Editing a book to make it sound succinct and clear is no easy feat. Combing through the text for a misplaced comma or hyphen is a job that very few people are good at. Thank you for elevating this work, and Gloria, the "texture" gave it life and emotion.

Jackie, Gloria, Rachel, Paul and Peter:

You are a constant support and inspiration to me. You are the apples of my eye. You are exactly the family I envisioned having - loud, opinionated, affectionate, and demanding, all at the same time. You have made me proud in more ways than I can count.

Jotham, Jeffrey, Chloe, Petra and Finley:

You, my grandchildren, have given me a second lease on life. I love you so much, and you make me the happiest grandfather in the world.

Worship At Joy Center:

Thank you for choosing me as your pastor, but most importantly, thank you for choosing me as your family.

Worship Harvest:

You have blessed me in more ways than I can count. I never dreamt that my legacy would involve a group as nation-changing as you are. Thank you for keeping me as your Uncle Ben. This book would not have been possible without you.

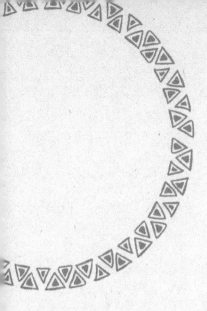

CPSIA information can be obtained
at www.ICGtesting.com
Printed in the USA
LVHW042049030322
712532LV00009B/617